THE WORLD WOULD BE A BETTER PLACE IF...

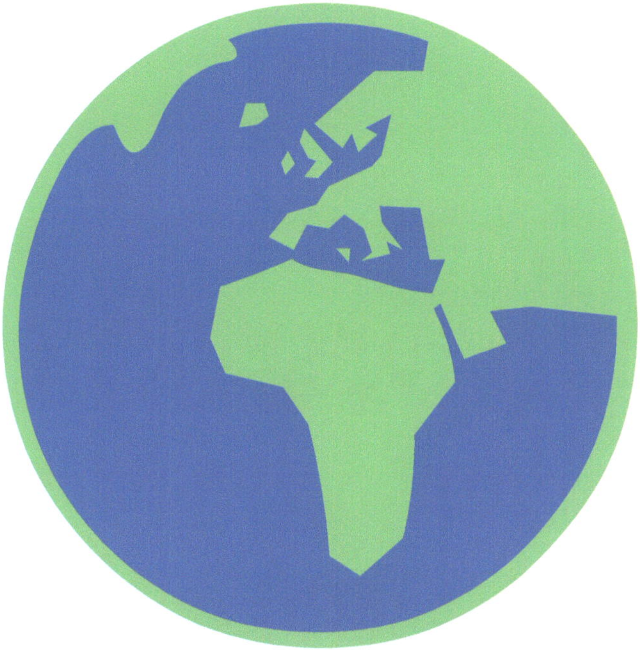

Mrs. McAuley's First Grade Class 2010–11

AuthorHouse™
1663 Liberty Drive
Bloomington, IN 47403
www.authorhouse.com
Phone: 1-800-839-8640

First published by AuthorHouse 2/23/2011

ISBN: 978-1-4567-3581-4 (sc)

Printed in the United States of America

Any people depicted in stock imagery provided by Thinkstock are models,
and such images are being used for illustrative purposes only.
Certain stock imagery © Thinkstock.

This book is printed on acid-free paper.

author HOUSE™

The WORLD WOULD be a better PLACE if...

families were together more often.

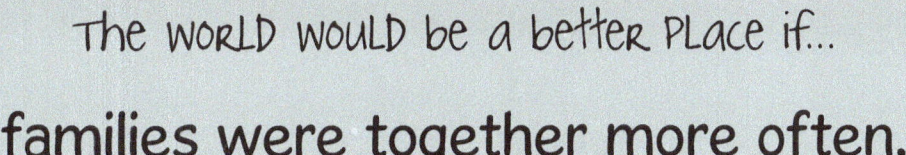

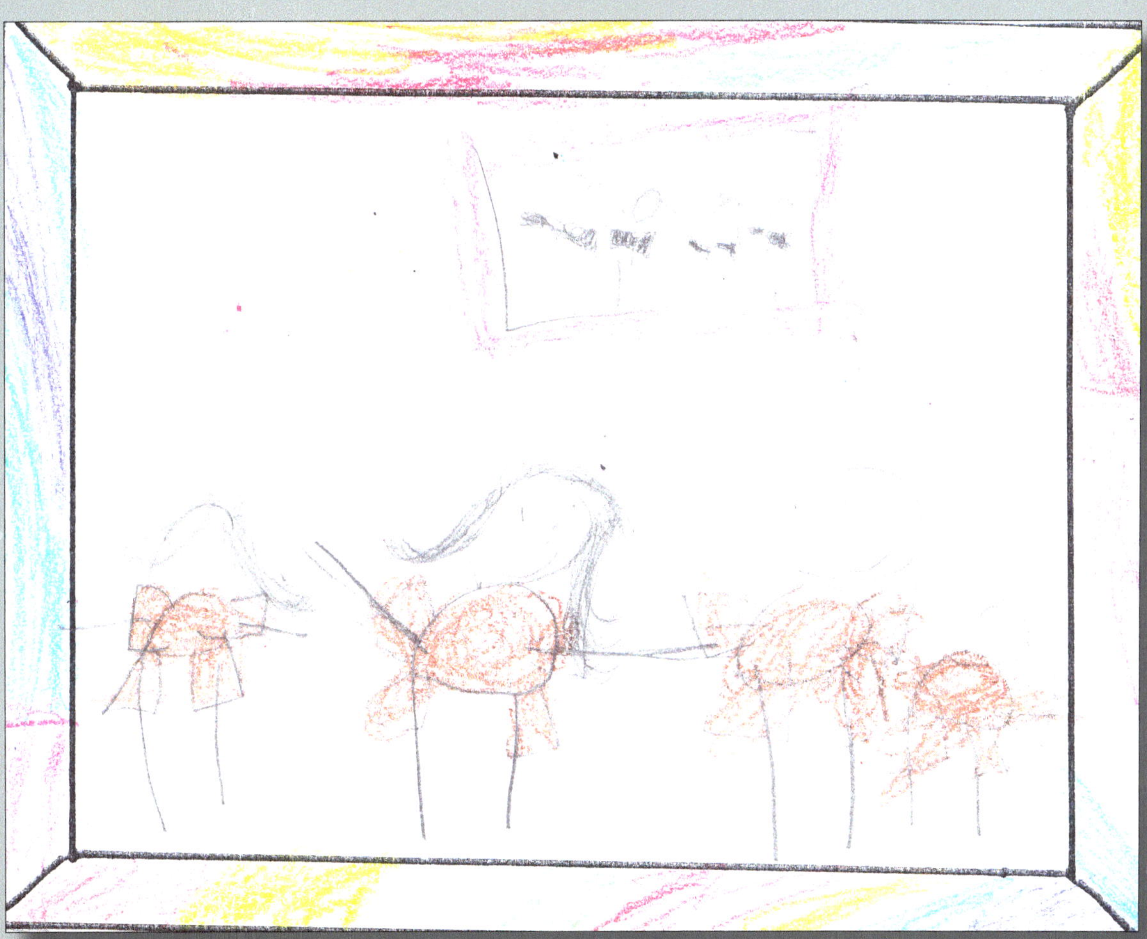

BY HALEY

The WORLD WOULD be a better PLACE if...

teachers played more with kids (more recess)!

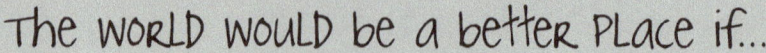

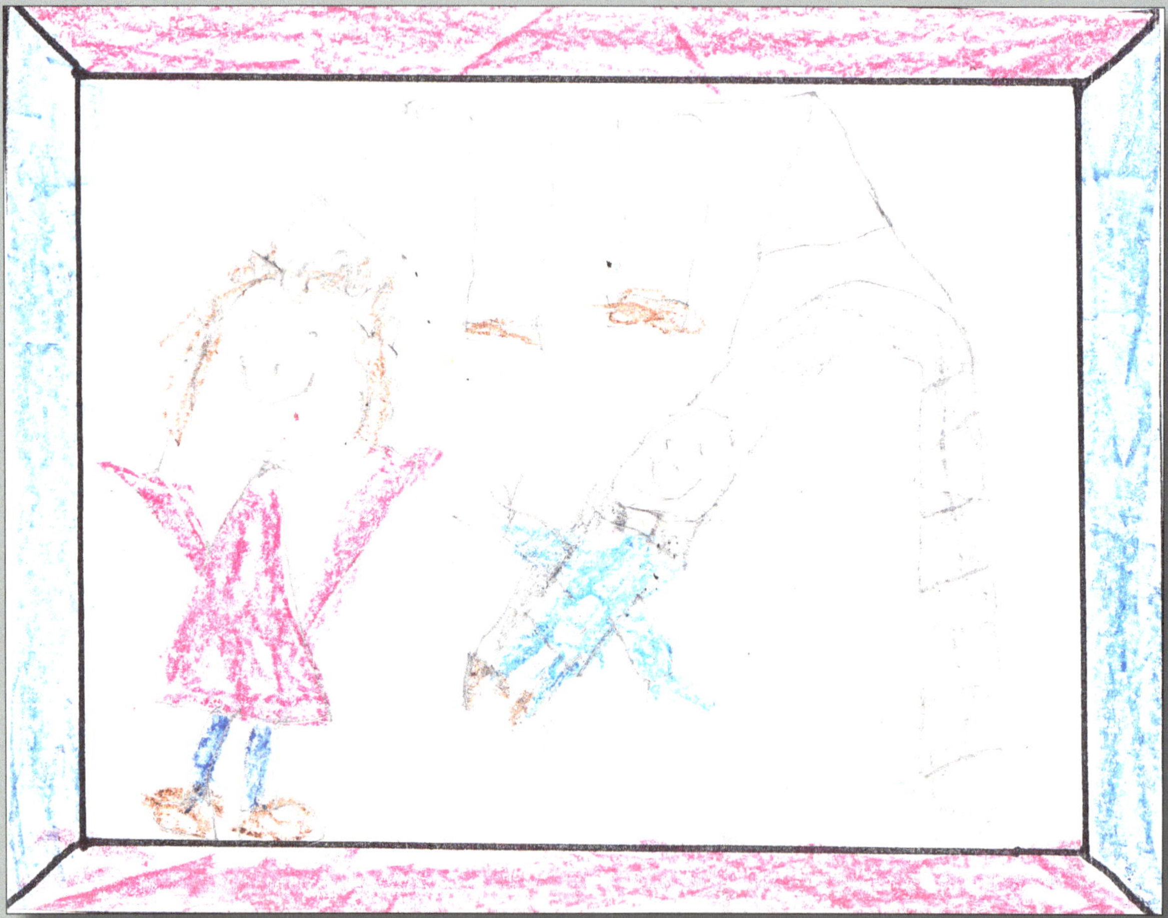

BY ETHAN

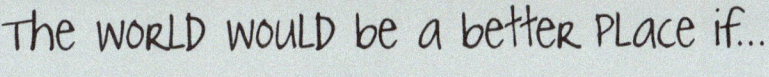

The WORLD WOULD be a better PLACE if...

kids cleaned up more.

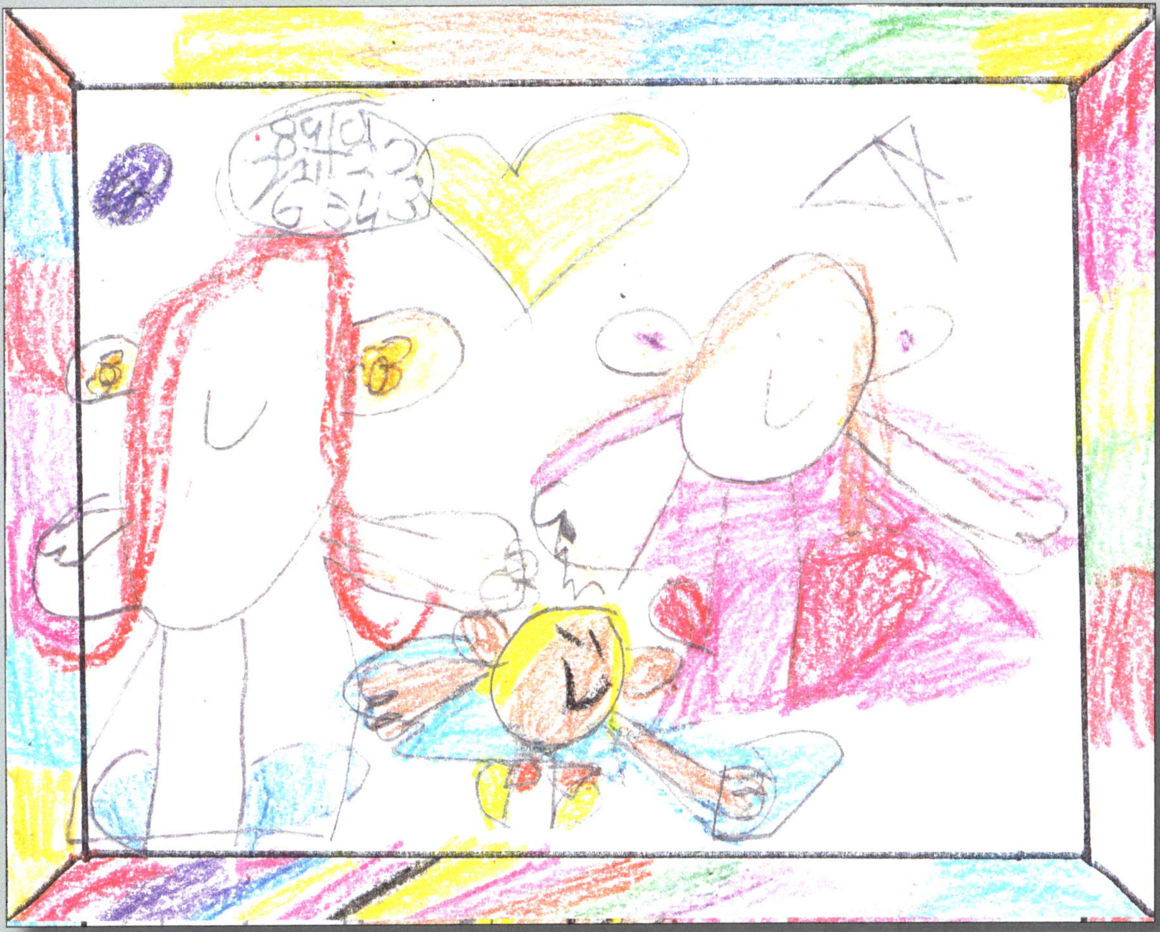

BY OLIVIA

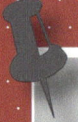
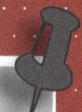

The WORLD WOULD be a better PLACE if...

we stayed healthy and lived longer.

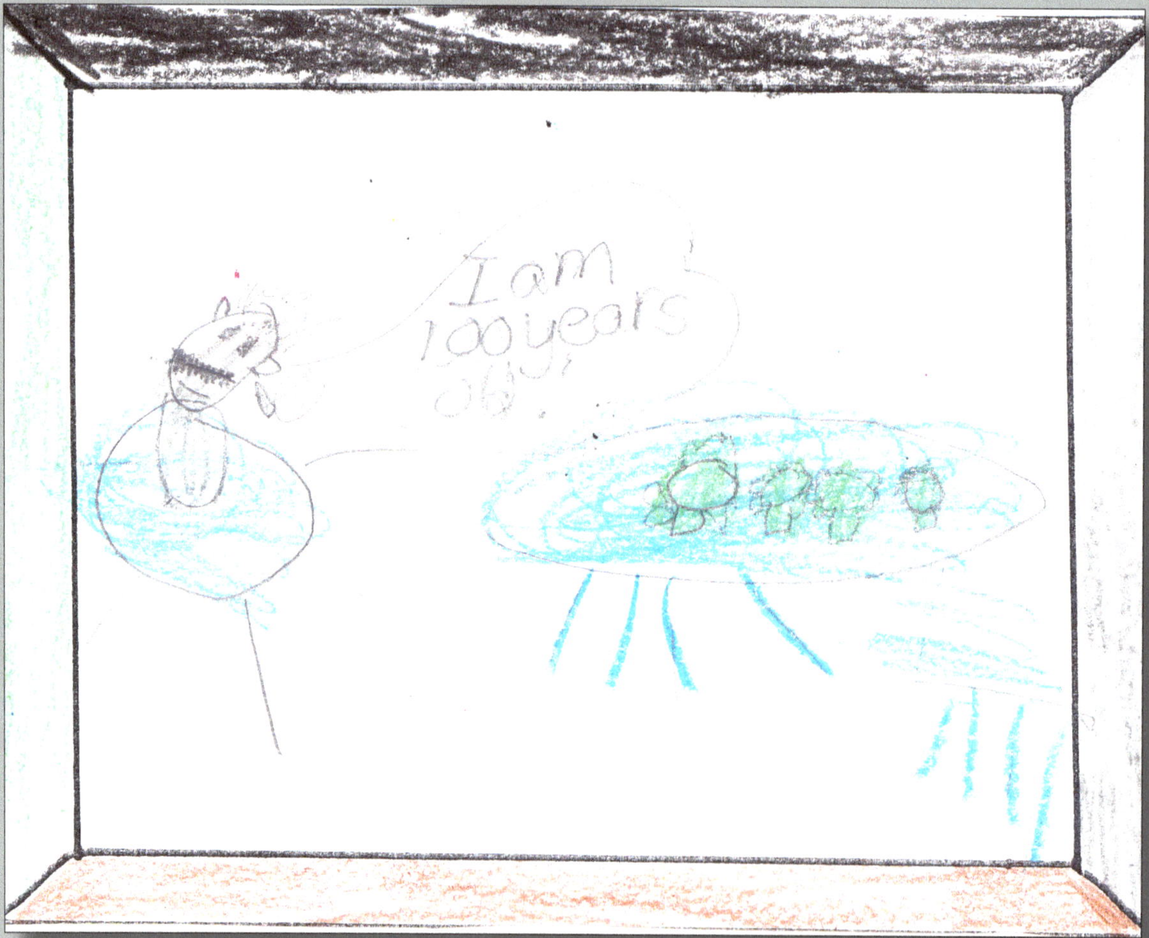

BY CALEB

The WORLD WOULD be a better PLACE if...

we recycled more.

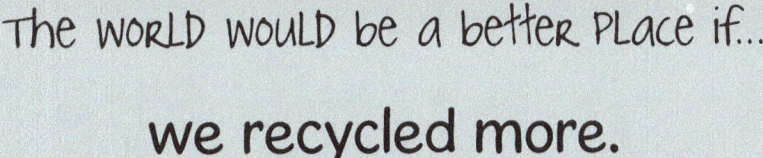

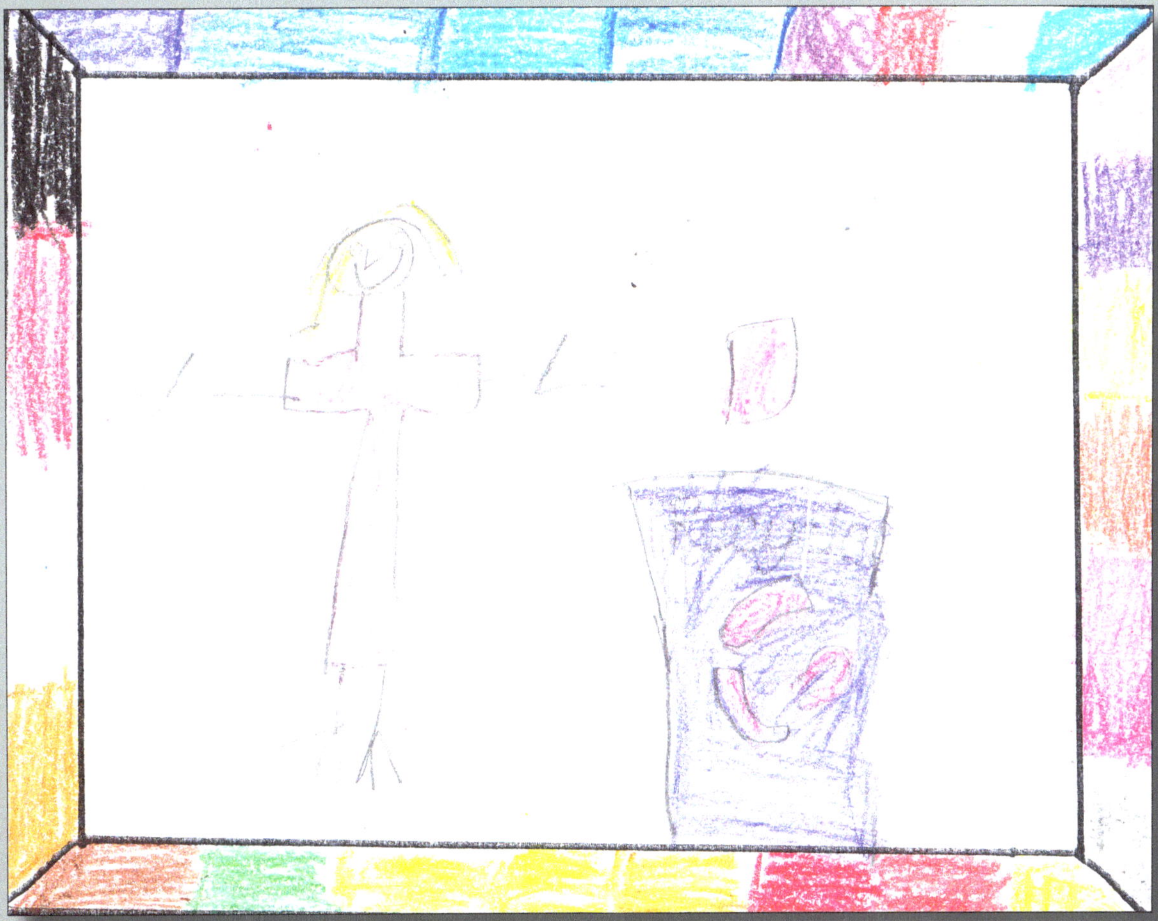

BY ASHLEY

The WORLD WOULD be a better PLACE if...

we helped animals more.

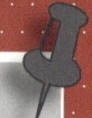

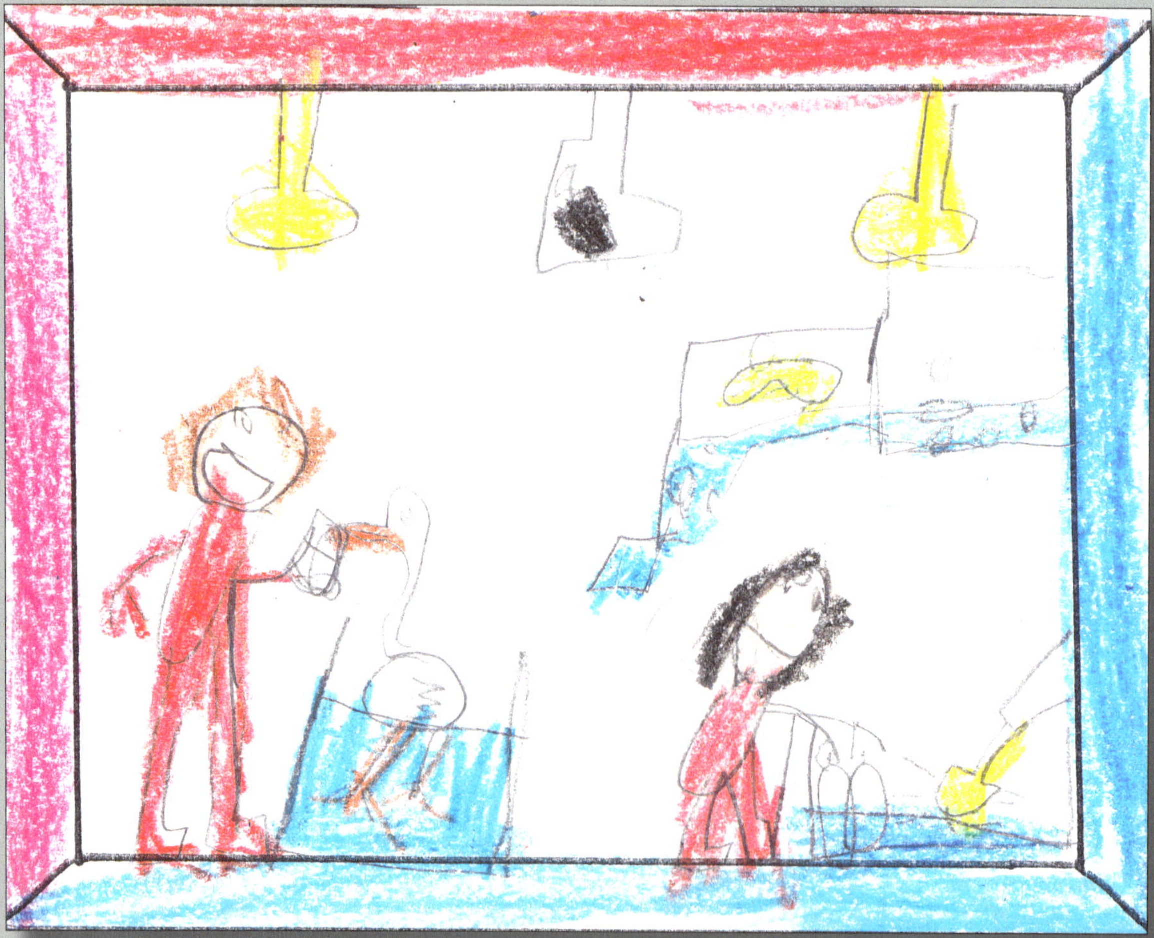

BY CAMERON

The WORLD WOULD be a better PLACE if...

we danced more.

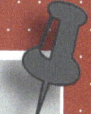

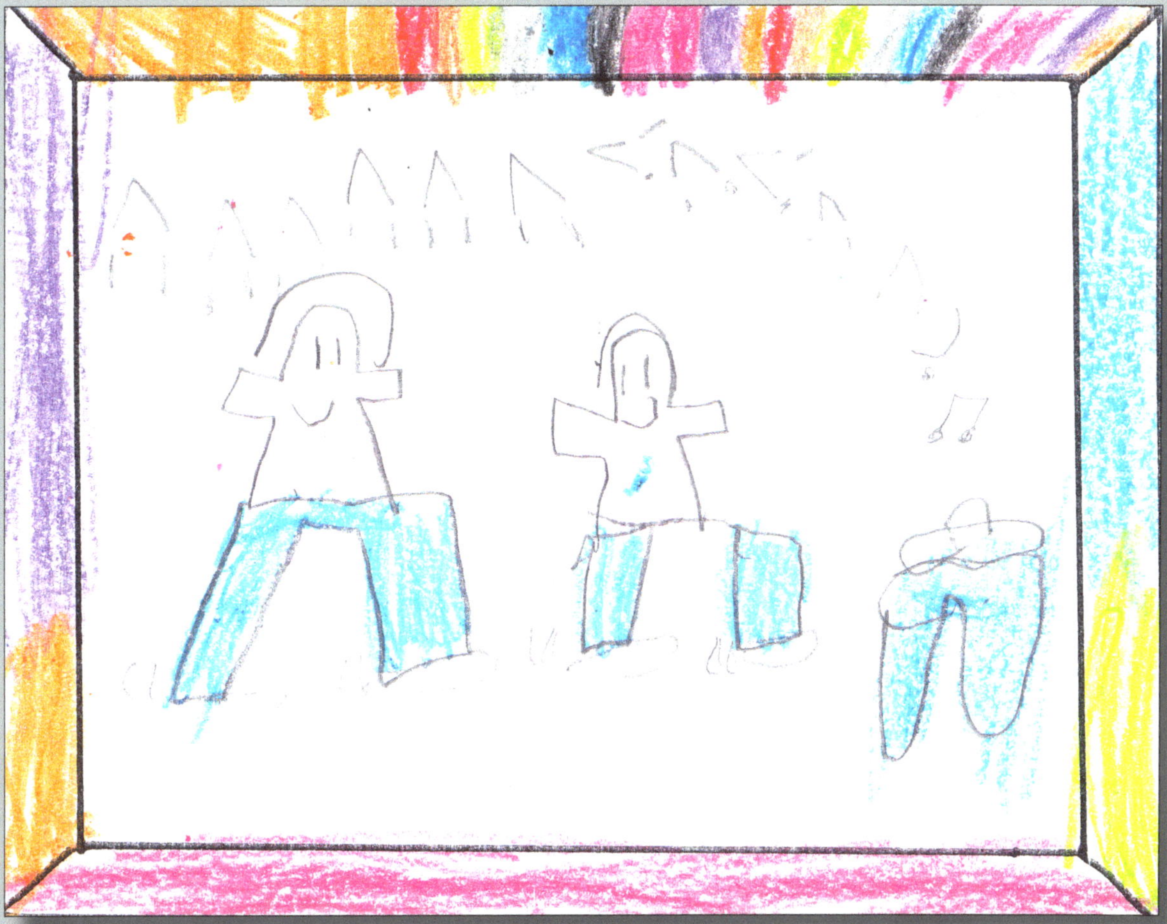

BY BELLA

The WORLD WOULD be a better PLACE if...

we could see wild animals and nature more often.

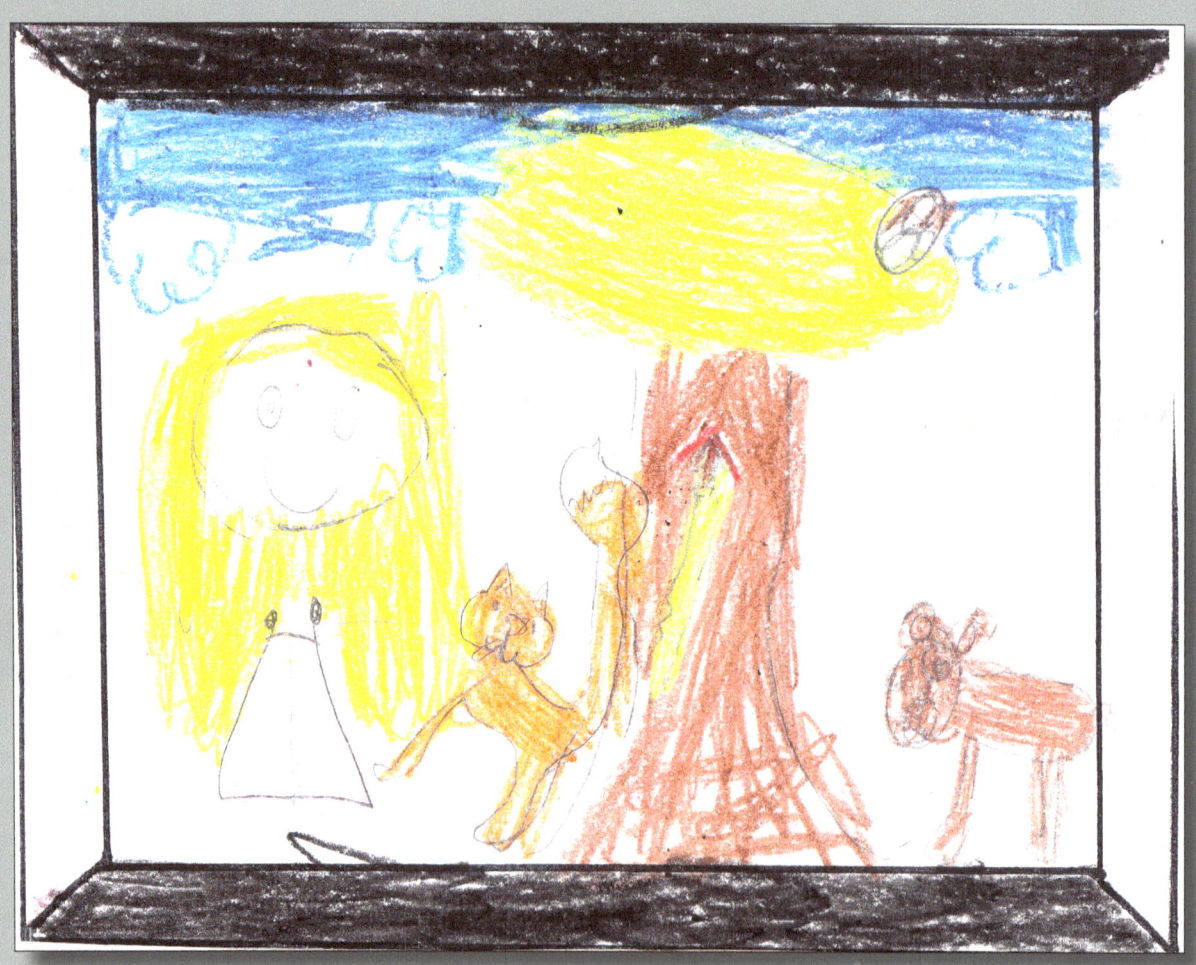

BY ALEXANDRIA

The WORLD WOULD be a better PLACE if...

it rained more (it has been very dry this year).

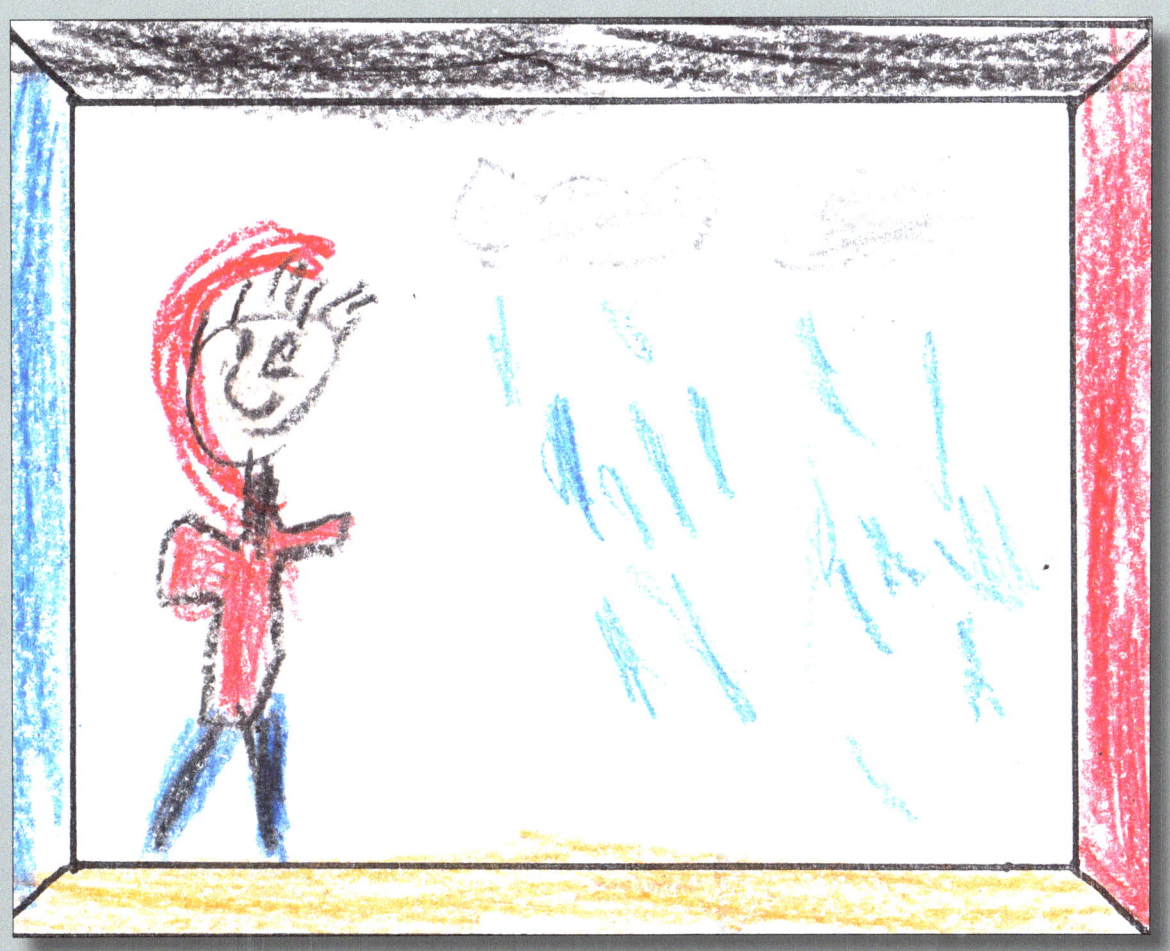

BY MATTHEW

The WORLD WOULD be a better PLACE if...

people had more time to rest.

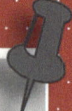

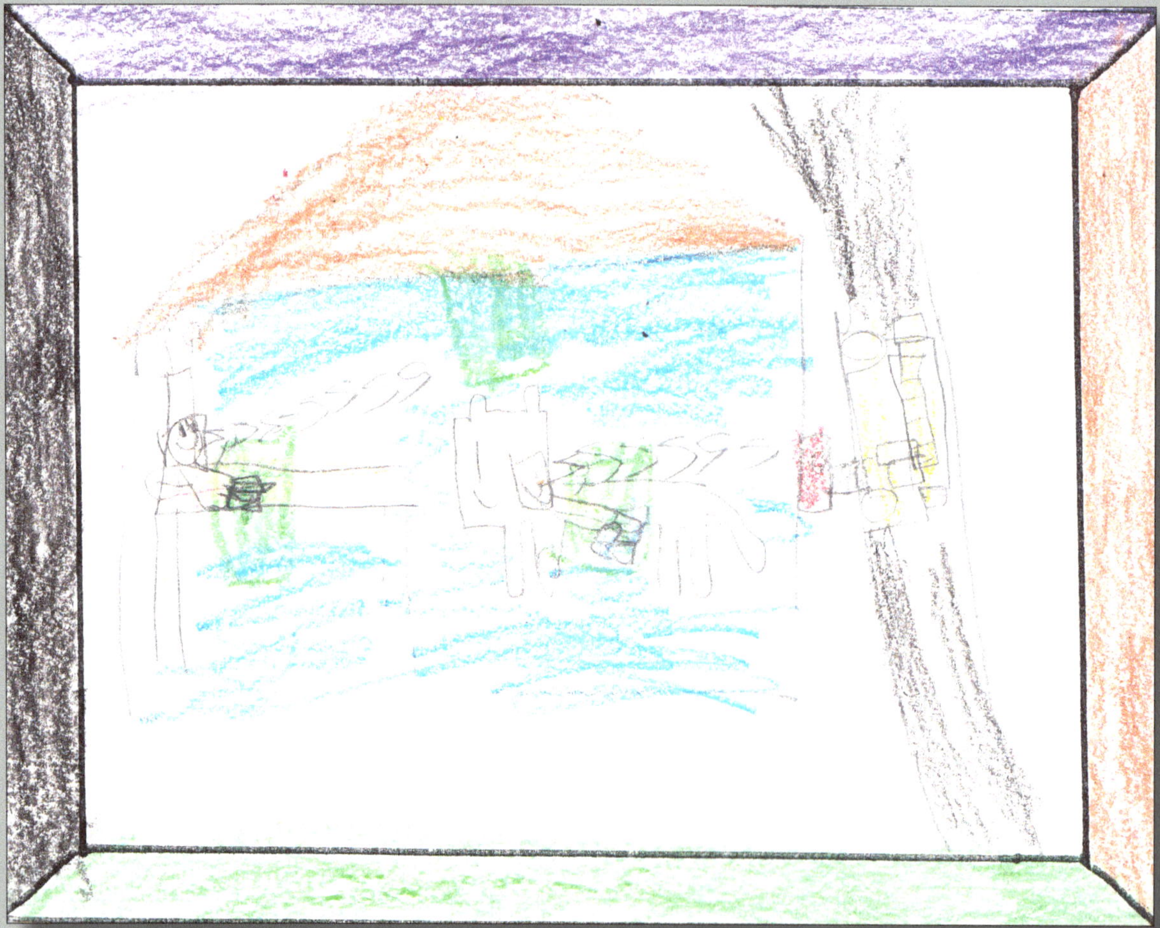

BY CHRIS

The WORLD WOULD be a better PLACE if...

the President gave people more stuff.

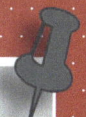

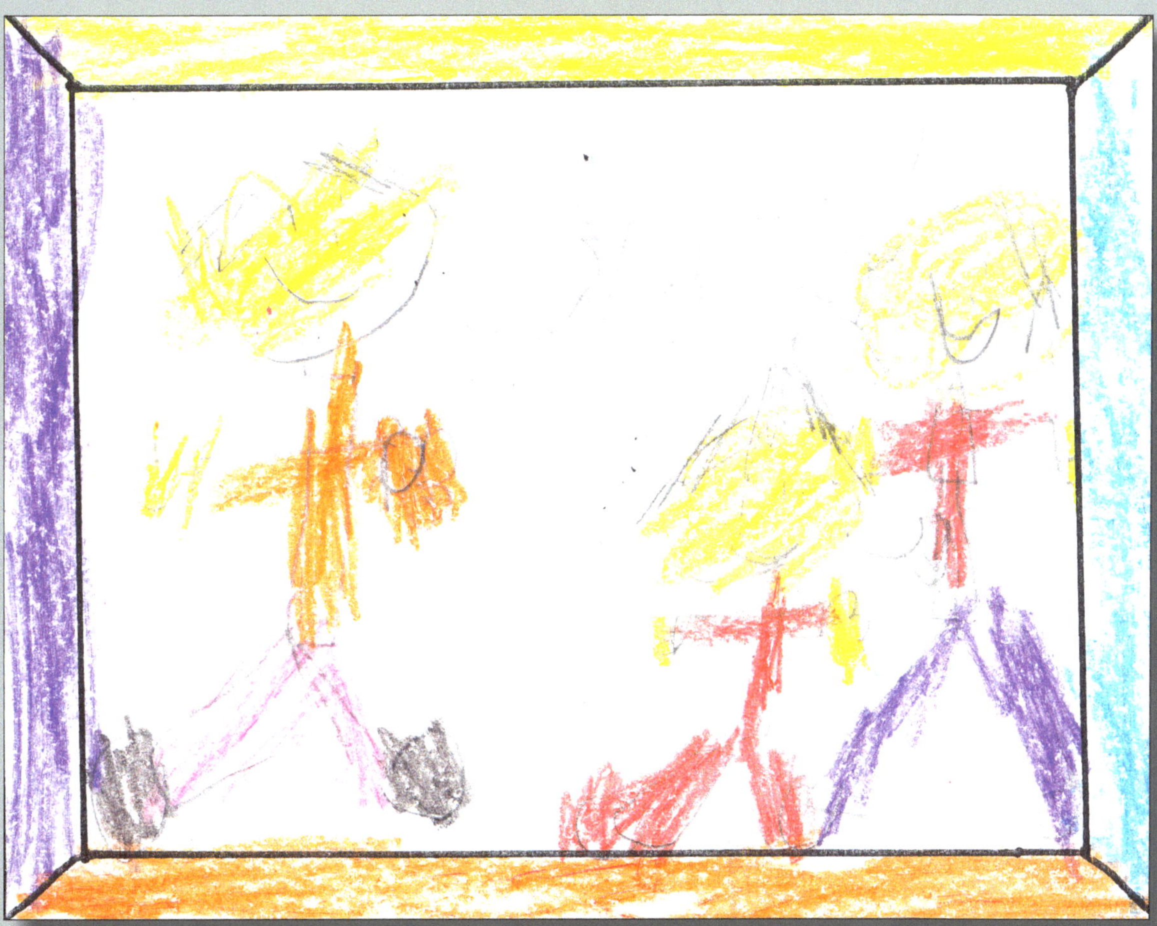

BY MARK

The WORLD WOULD be a better PLace if...

parents helped kids clean their room more.

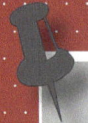
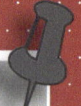

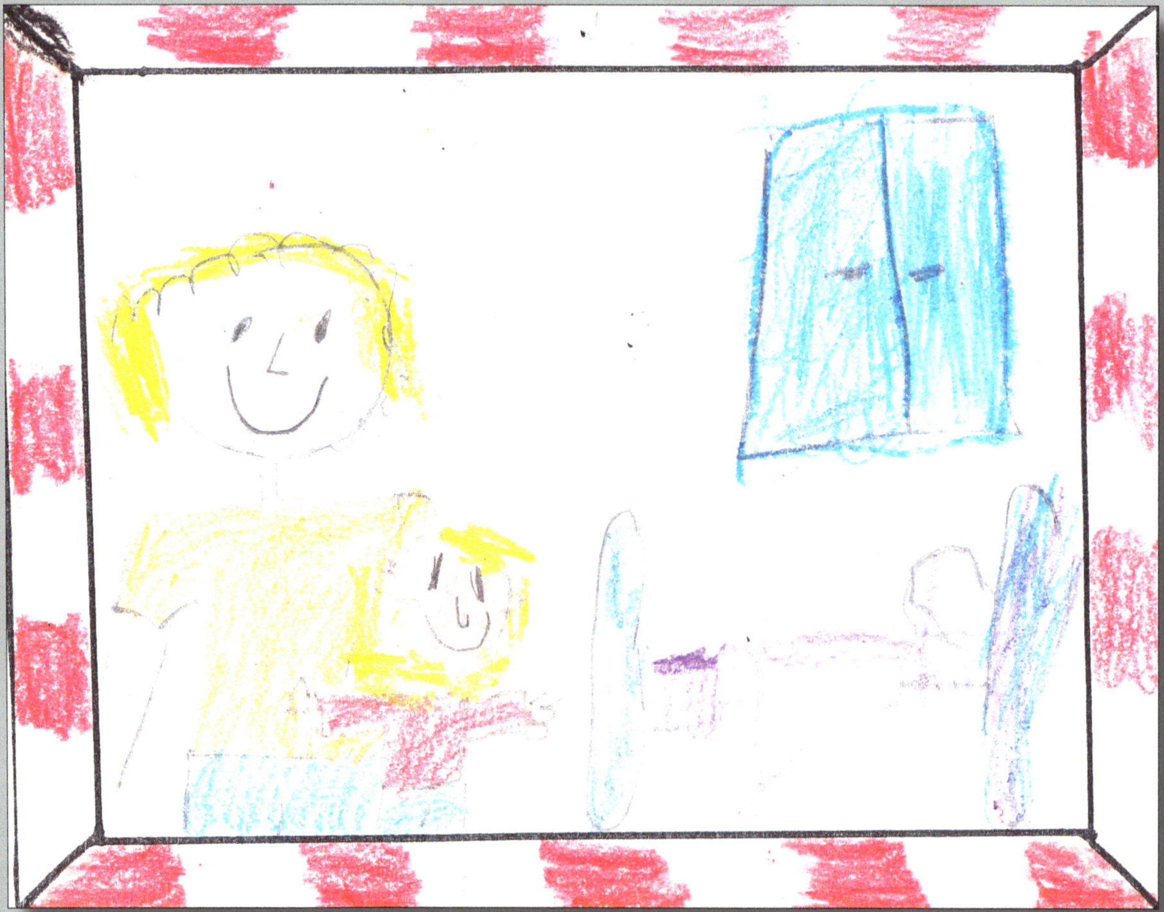

BY HANNAH

The WORLD WOULD be a better PLACE if...

we had breakfast with the principal every day.

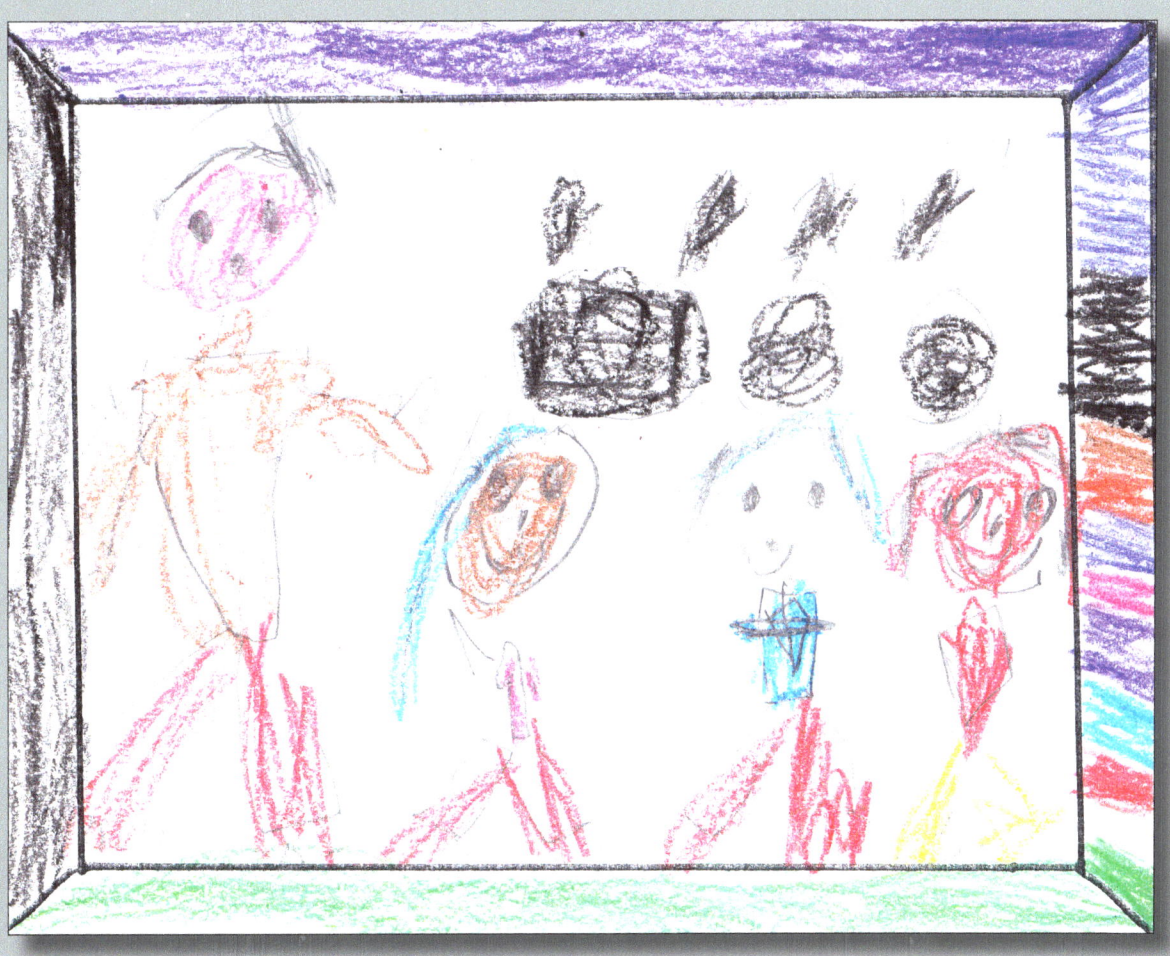

BY COOPER

The WORLD WOULD be a better PLACE if...

we had Pajama Day every day.

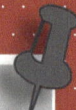

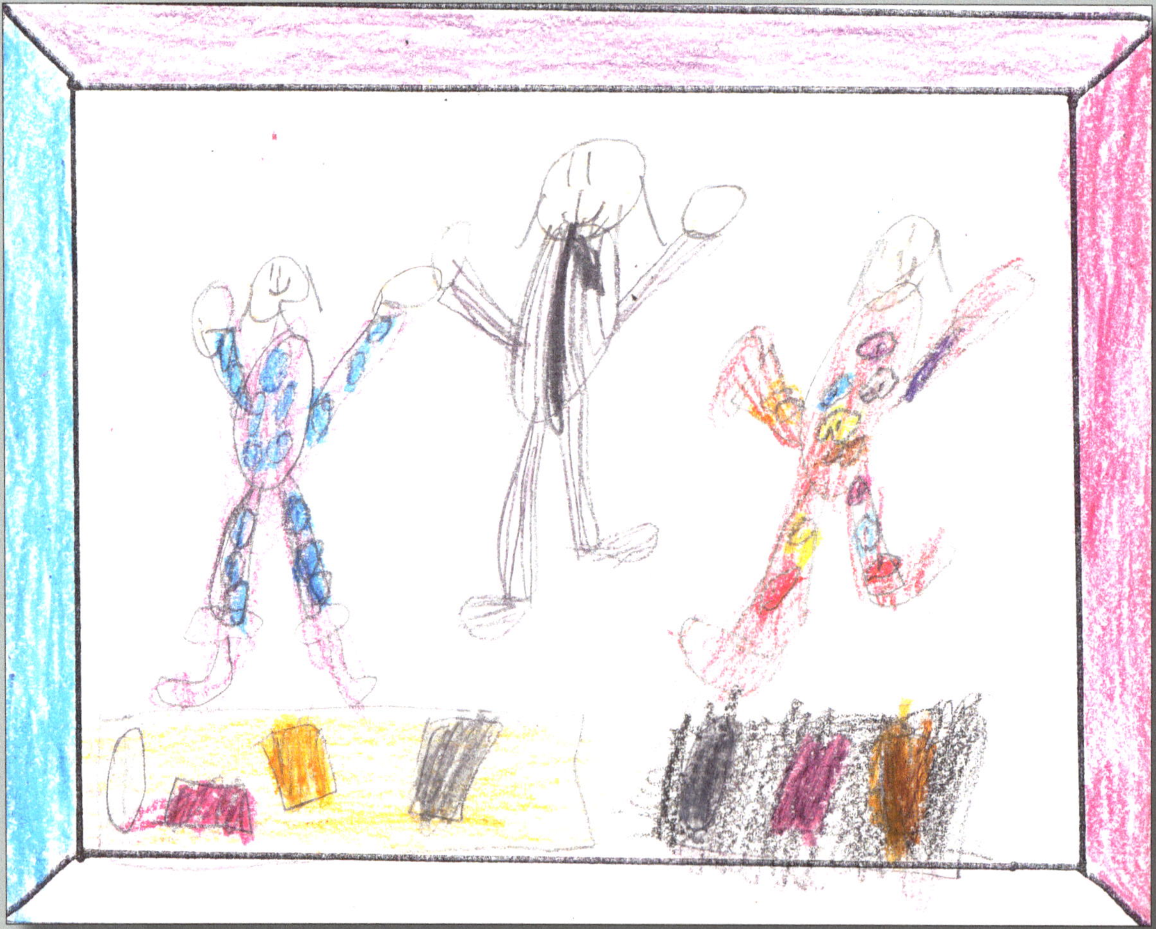

BY MAGGIE

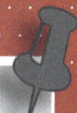

The WORLD WOULD be a better PLACE if...

we jumped on the trampoline more.

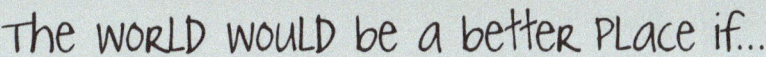

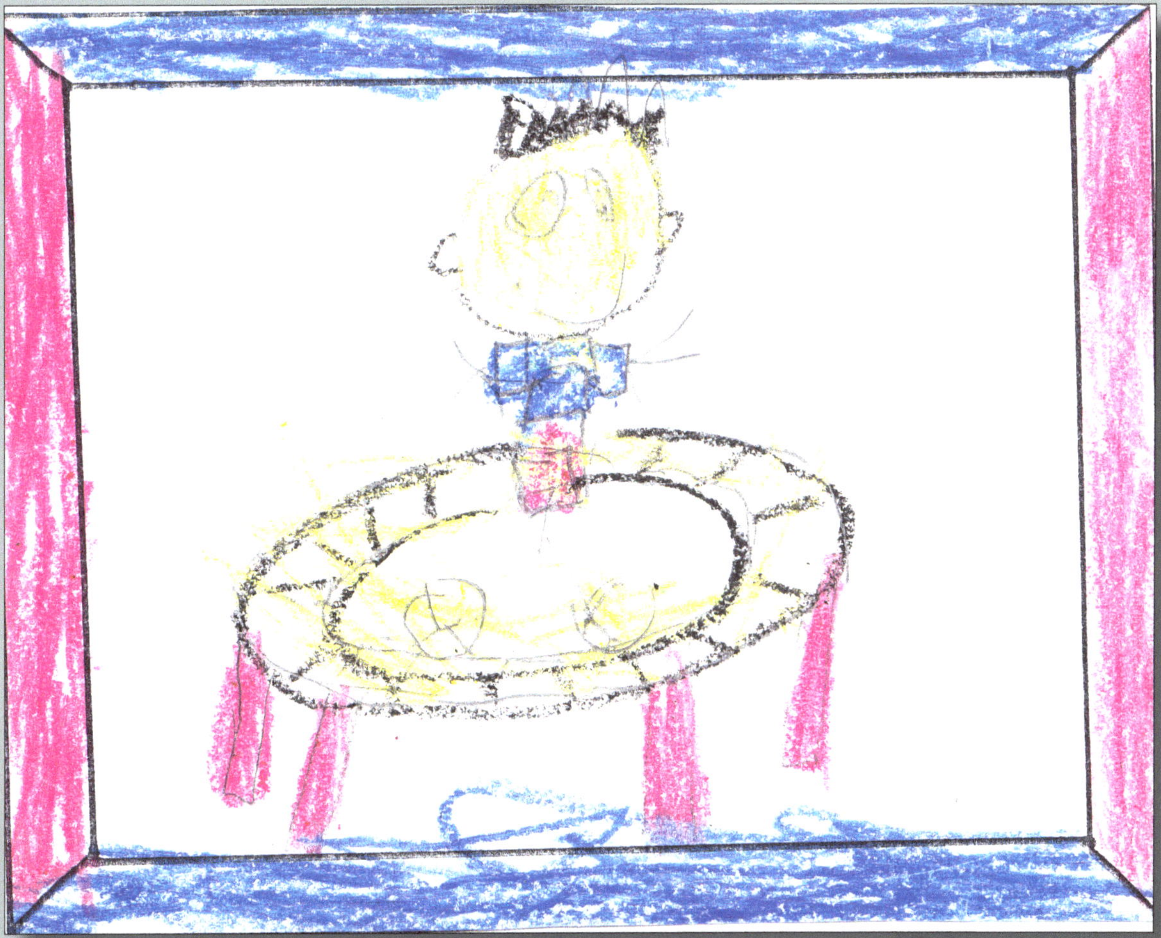

BY HUNTER

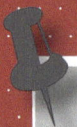
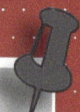

The WORLD WOULD be a better PLACE if...

adults were a little silly sometimes.

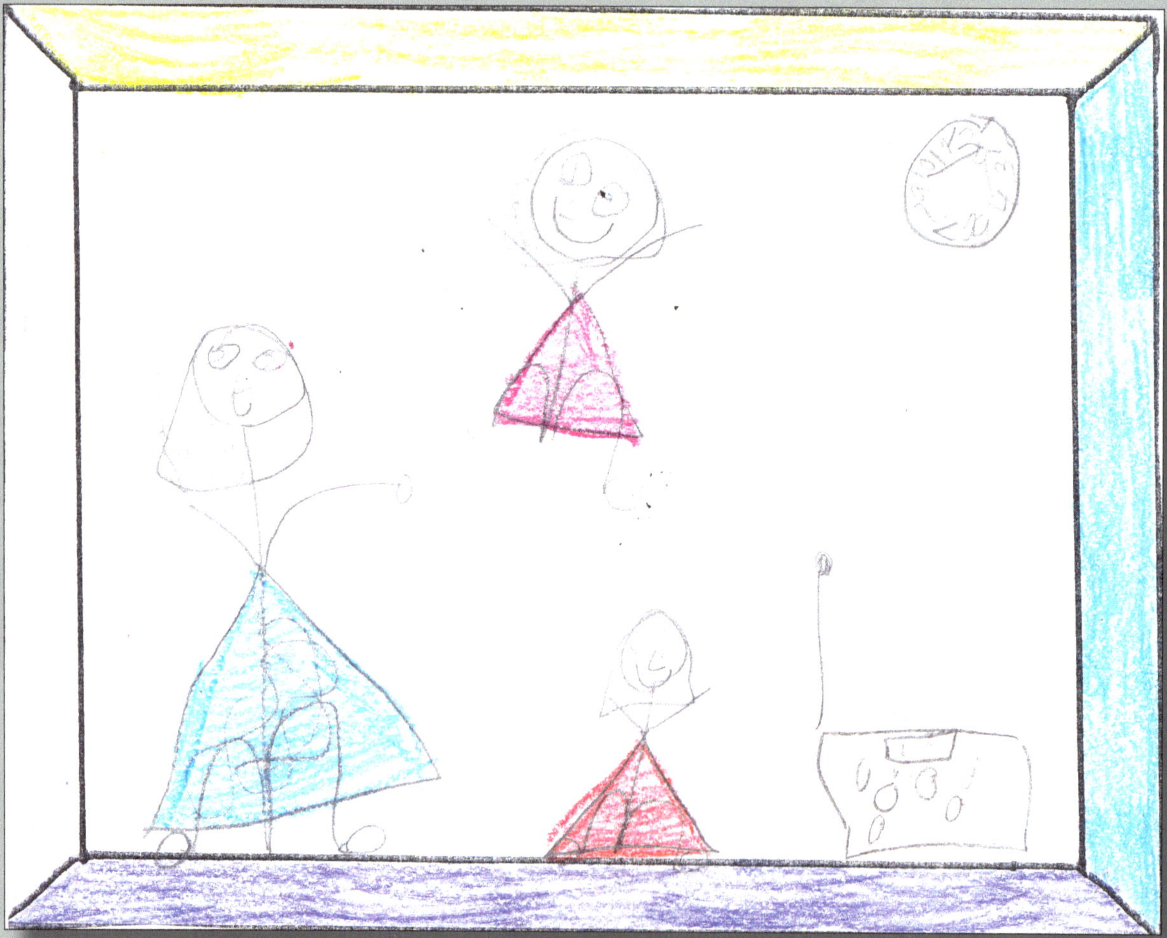

BY EMMA

The WORLD WOULD be a better PLACE if...

we exercised more.

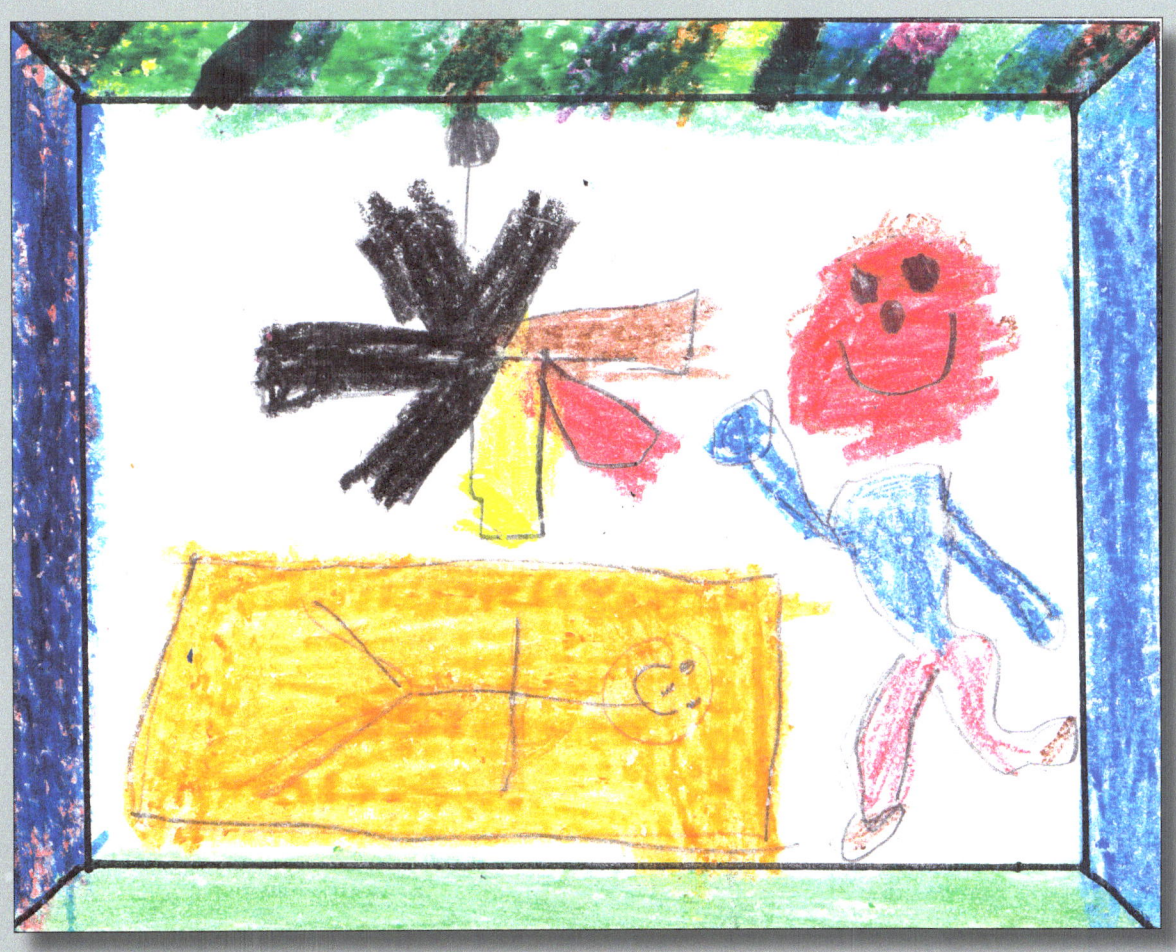

BY BRAEDEN

The WORLD WOULD be a better PLACE if...

teachers had sleepovers with kids.

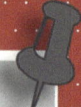

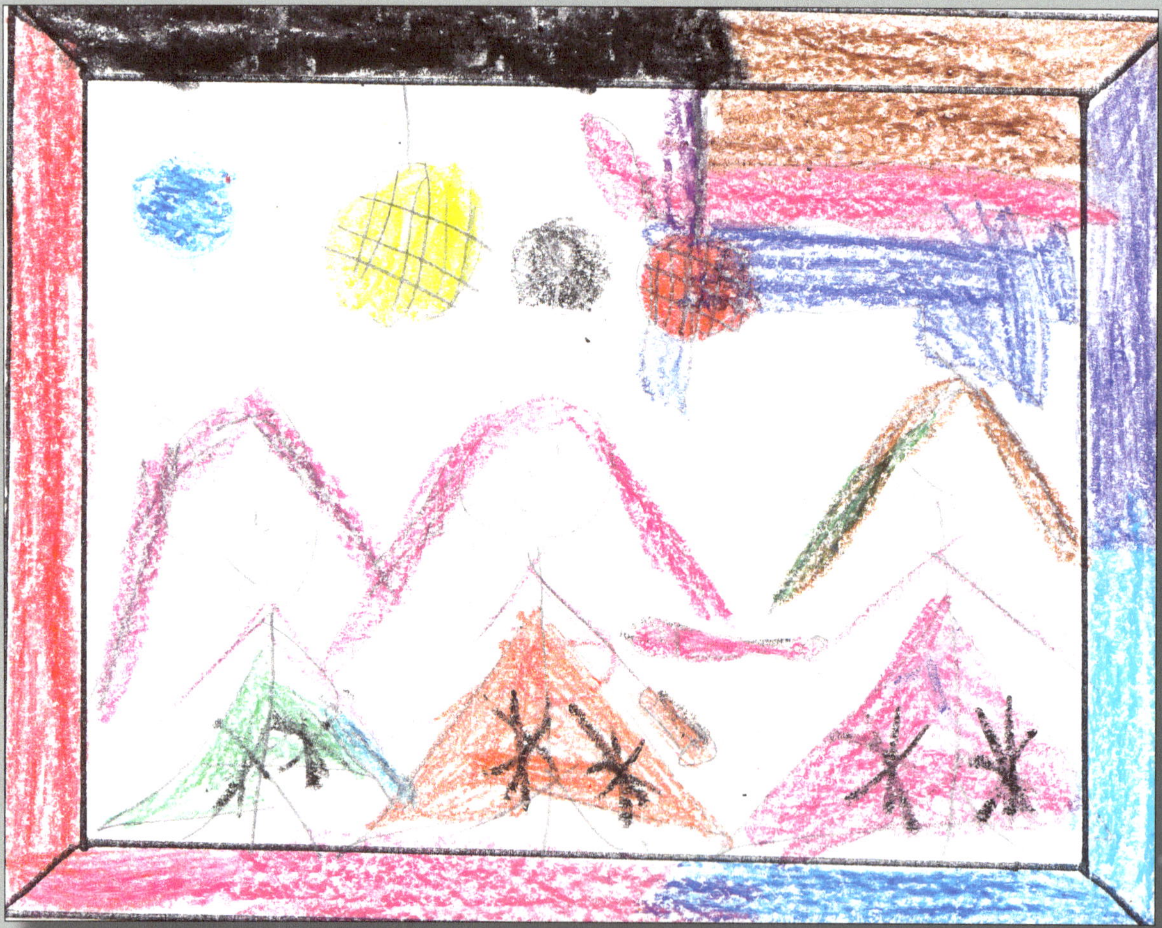

BY MEAGHAN

The WORLD WOULD be a better PLACE if...

we did more science experiments.

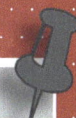

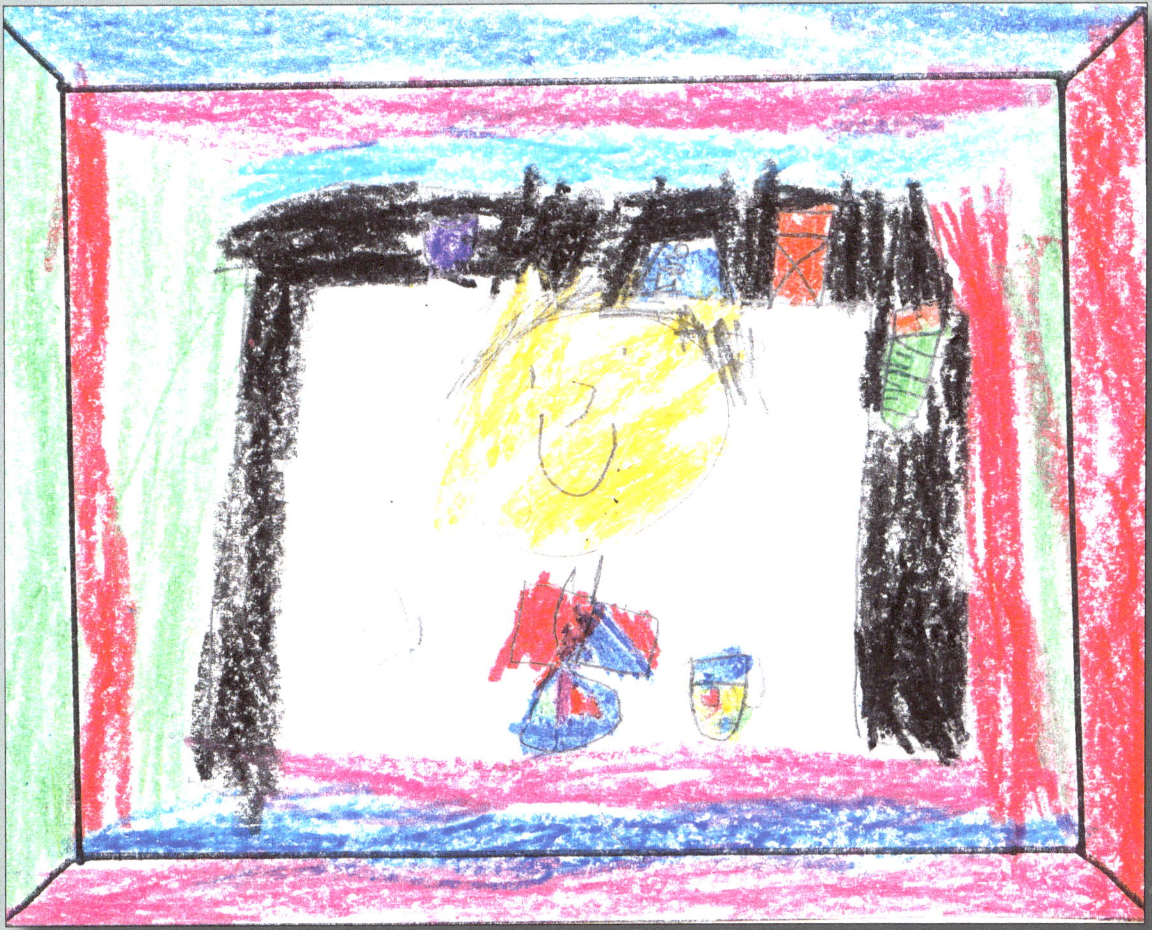

BY HOUSTON

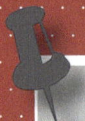
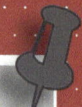

The WORLD WOULD be a better PLACE if...

kids could stay up longer.

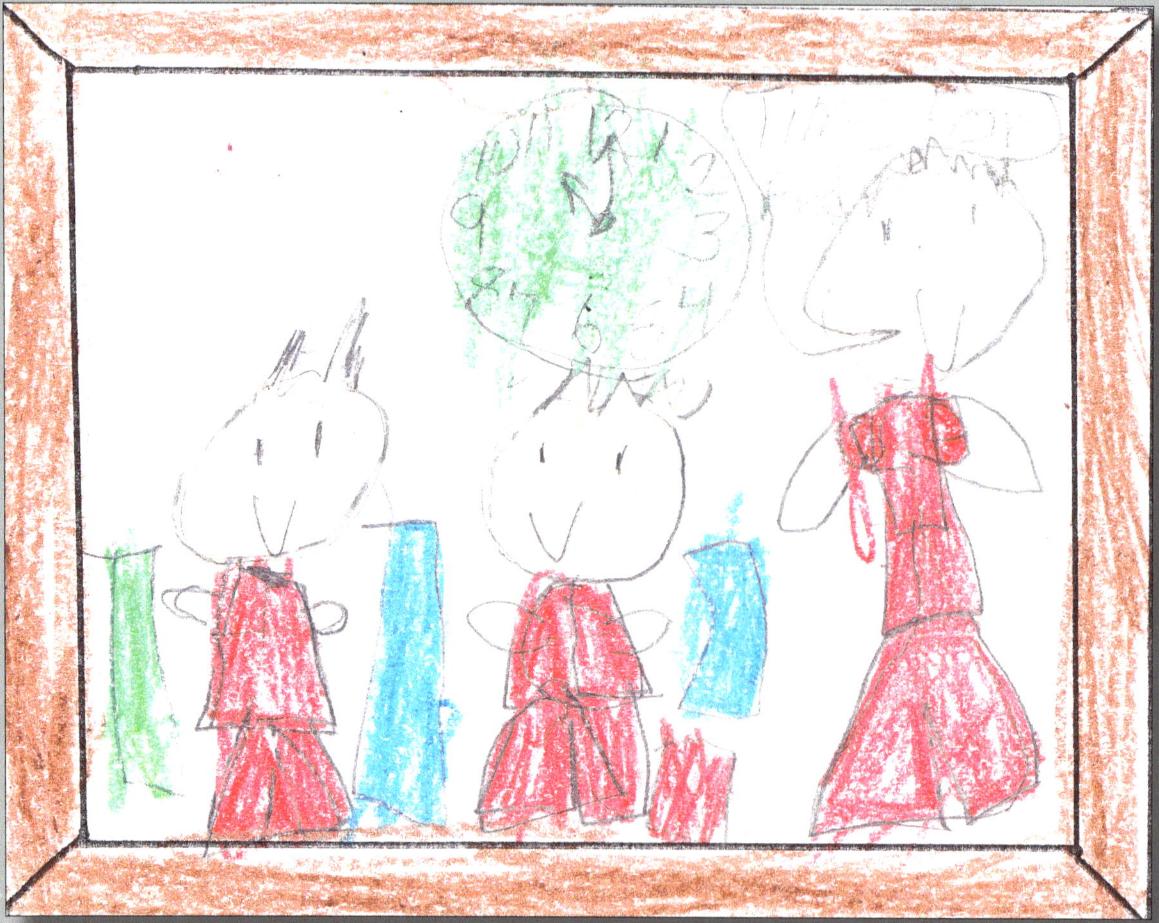

BY J.D. (JAMES)

The WORLD WOULD be a better PLACE if...

there were more of you in it.

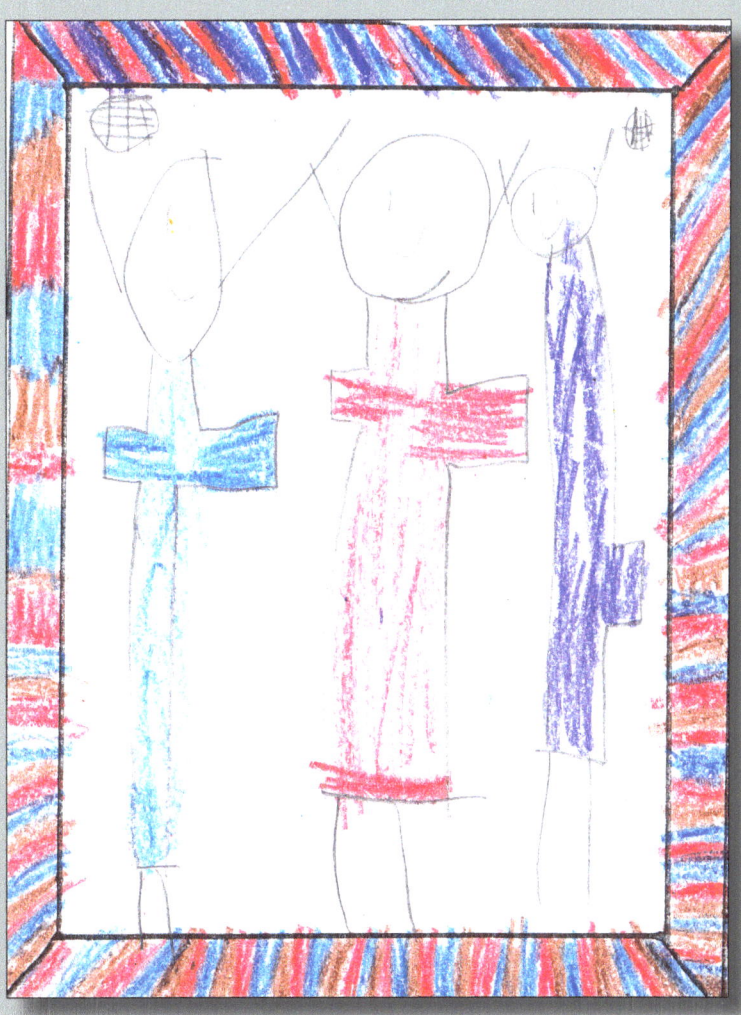

BY LEXI

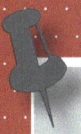
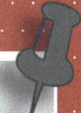

Authors and Illustrators

Matthew A.

Hunter A.

J.D. James A.

Cooper A.

Emma B.

Caleb B.

Houston B.

Cameron C.

Meaghan C.

Olivia D.

Hannah E.

Ethan G.

Ashley G.

Chris M.

Haley M.

Bella M.

Lexi N.

Maggie P.

Braeden P.

Alexandria R.

Mark S.

www.ingramcontent.com/pod-product-compliance
Lightning Source LLC
Chambersburg PA
CBHW050829200526
R18329200001B/R183292PG45159CBX00001B/1

THE WORLD WOULD BE A BETTER PLACE IF...

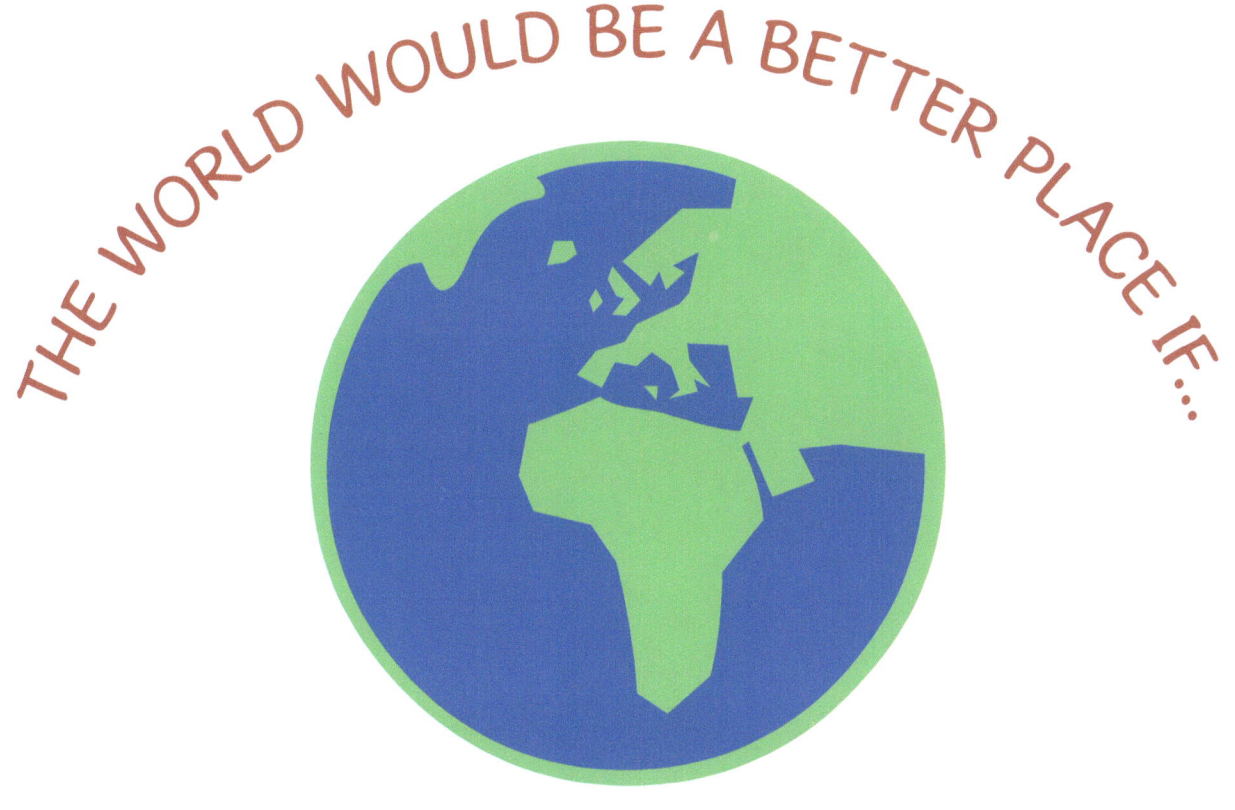

Mrs. McAuley's First Grade Class 2010-11

AuthorHouse™
1663 Liberty Drive
Bloomington, IN 47403
www.authorhouse.com
Phone: 1-800-839-8640

First published by AuthorHouse 2/23/2011

ISBN: 978-1-4567-3581-4 (sc)

Printed in the United States of America

authorHOUSE

The WORLD WOULD be a better PLACE if...

families were together more often.

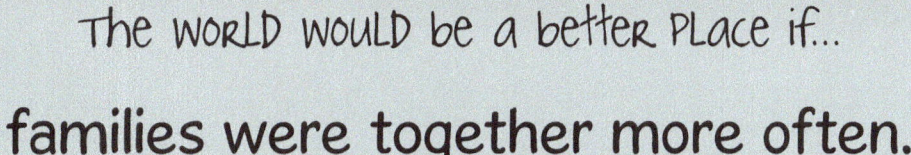

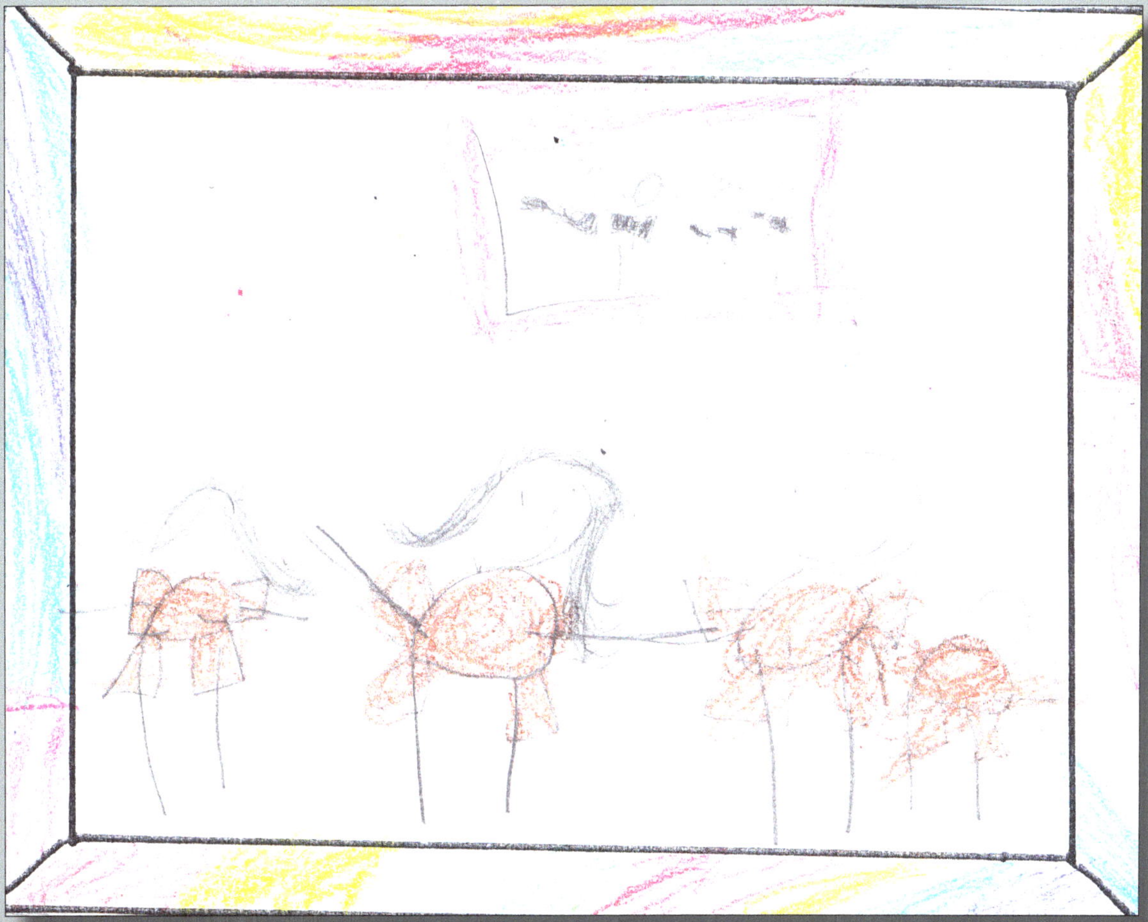

BY HALEY

The WORLD WOULD be a better PLaCe if...

teachers played more with kids (more recess)!

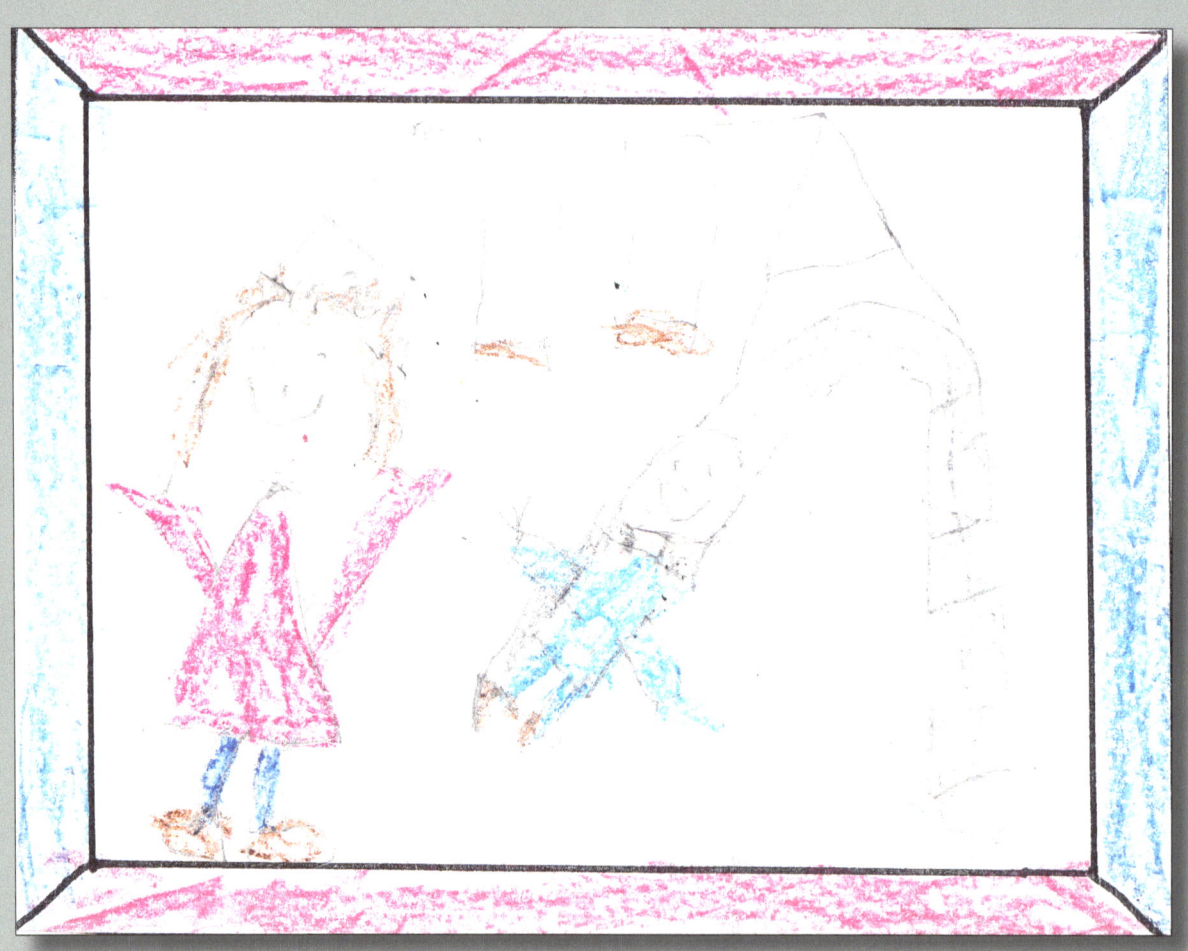

BY ETHAN

The WORLD WOULD be a better PLACE if...

kids cleaned up more.

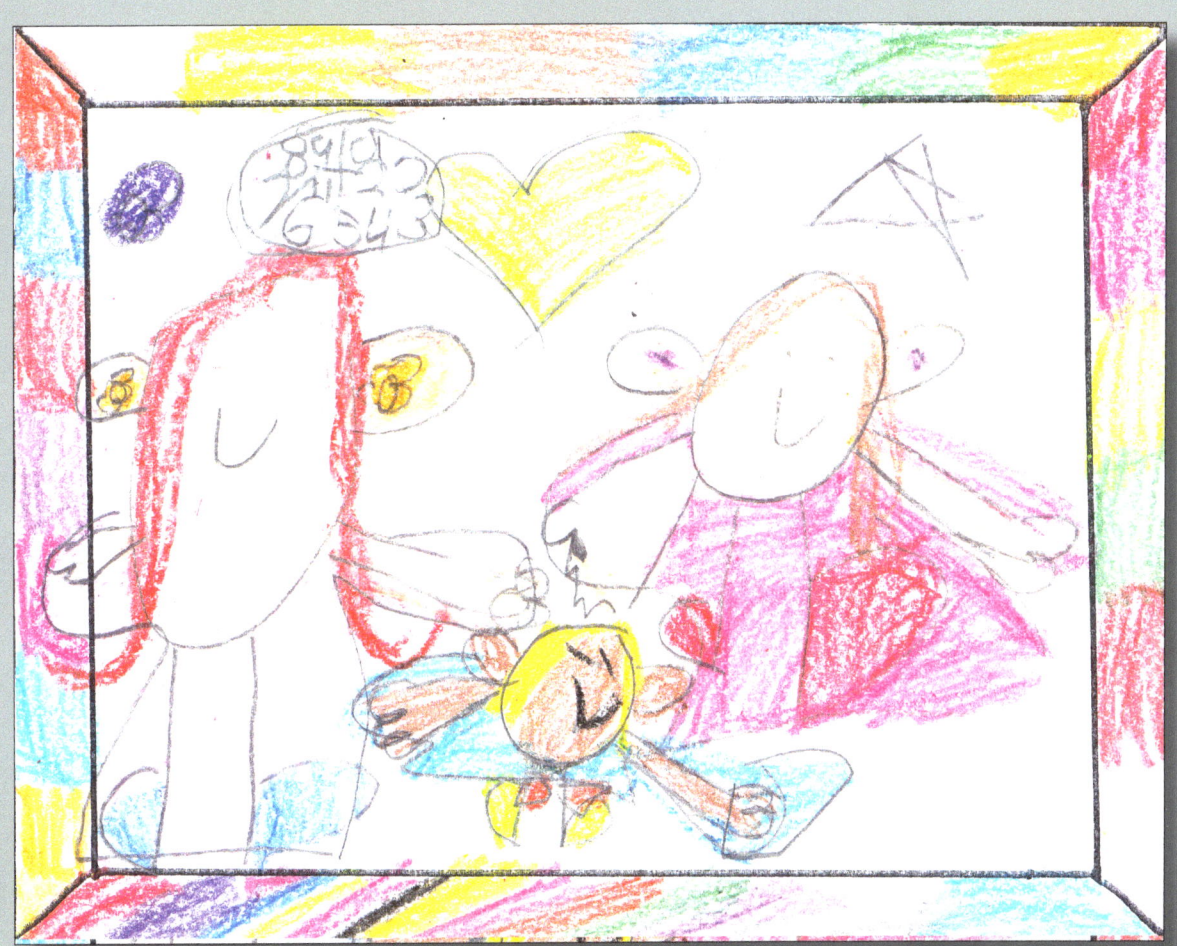

BY OLIVIA

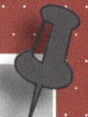

The WORLD WOULD be a better PLACE if...

we stayed healthy and lived longer.

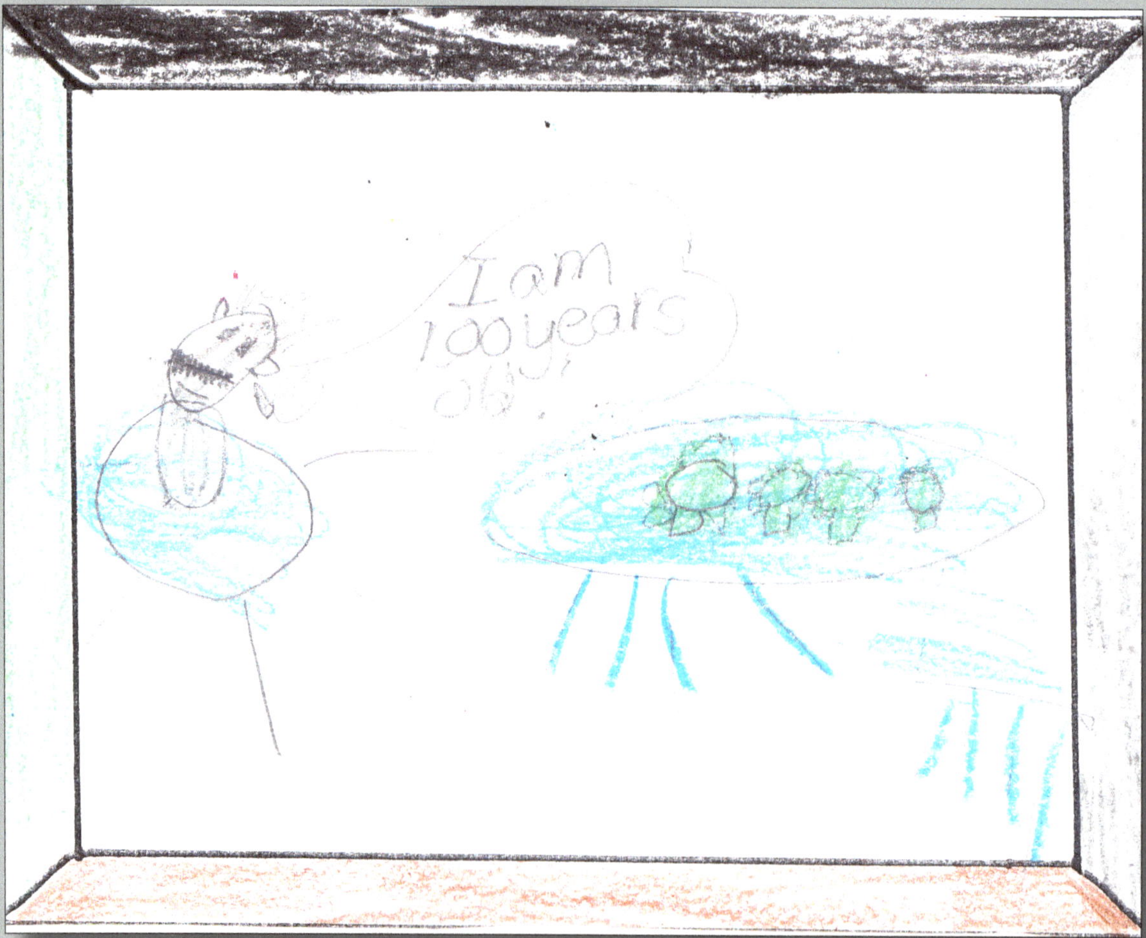

BY CALEB

The WORLD WOULD be a better PLACE if...

we recycled more.

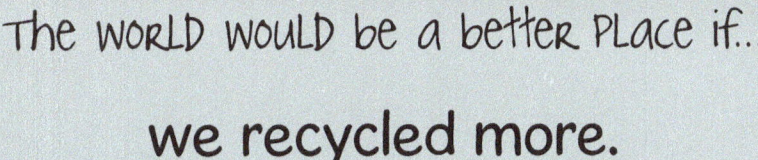

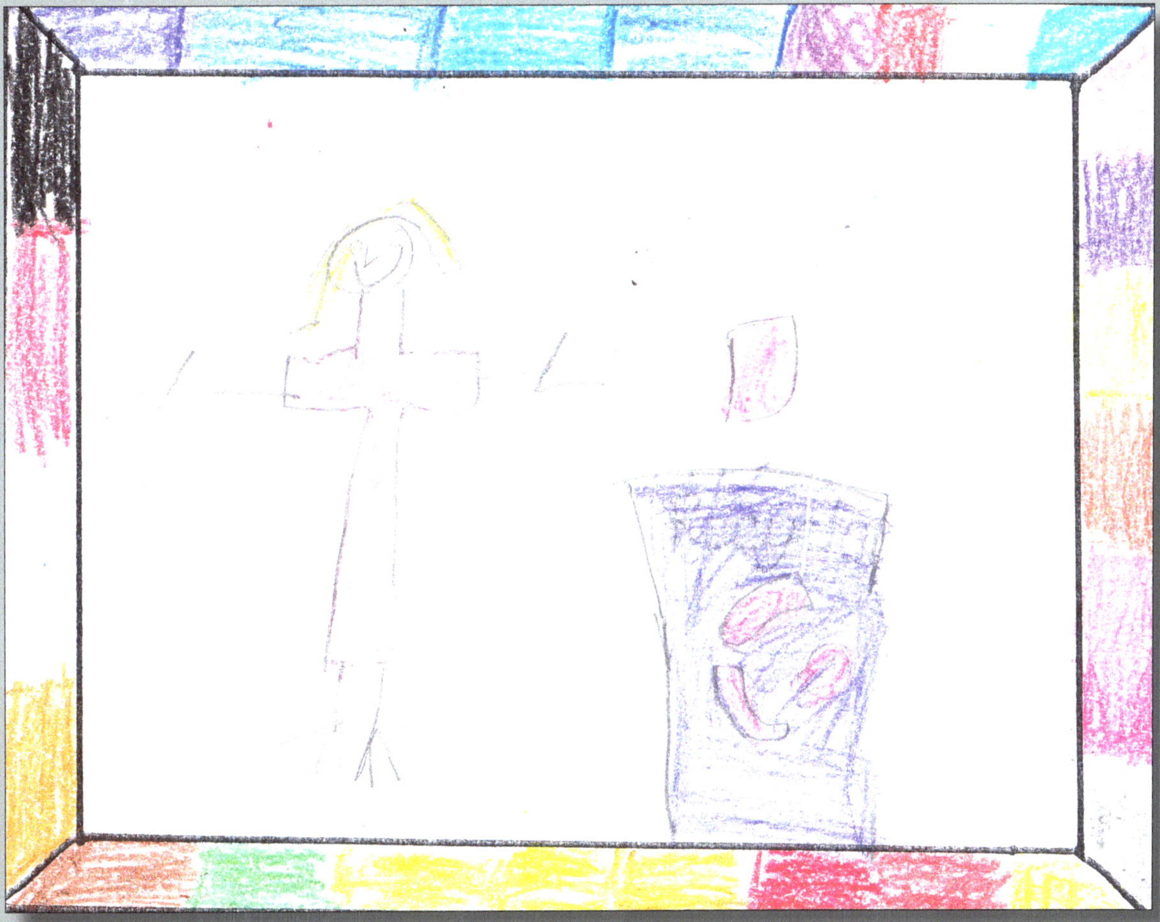

BY ASHLEY

The WORLD WOULD be a better PLACE if...

we helped animals more.

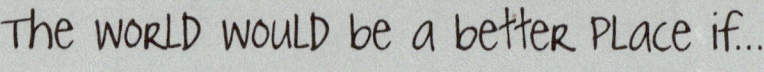

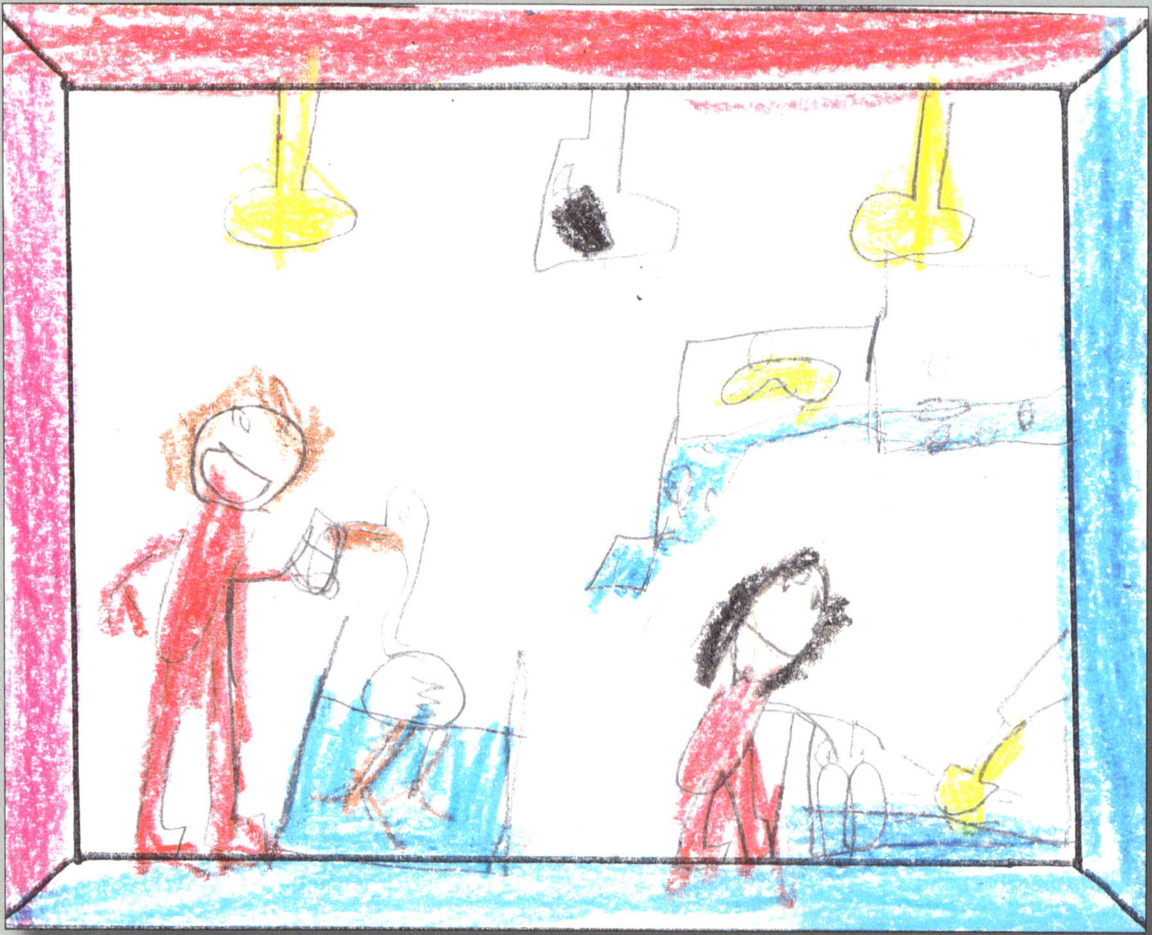

BY CAMERON

The WORLD WOULD be a better PLACE if...

we danced more.

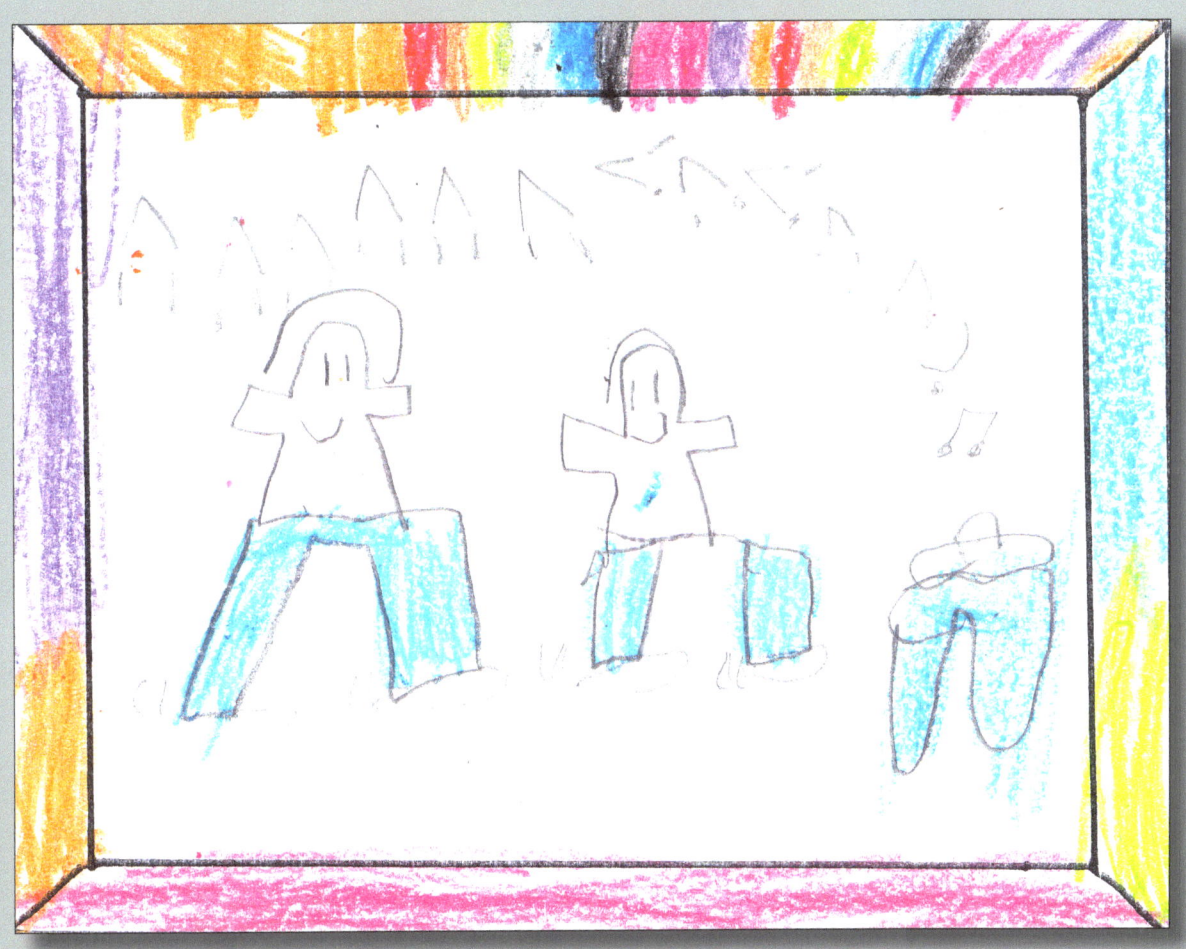

BY BELLA

The WORLD WOULD be a better PLACE if...

we could see wild animals and nature more often.

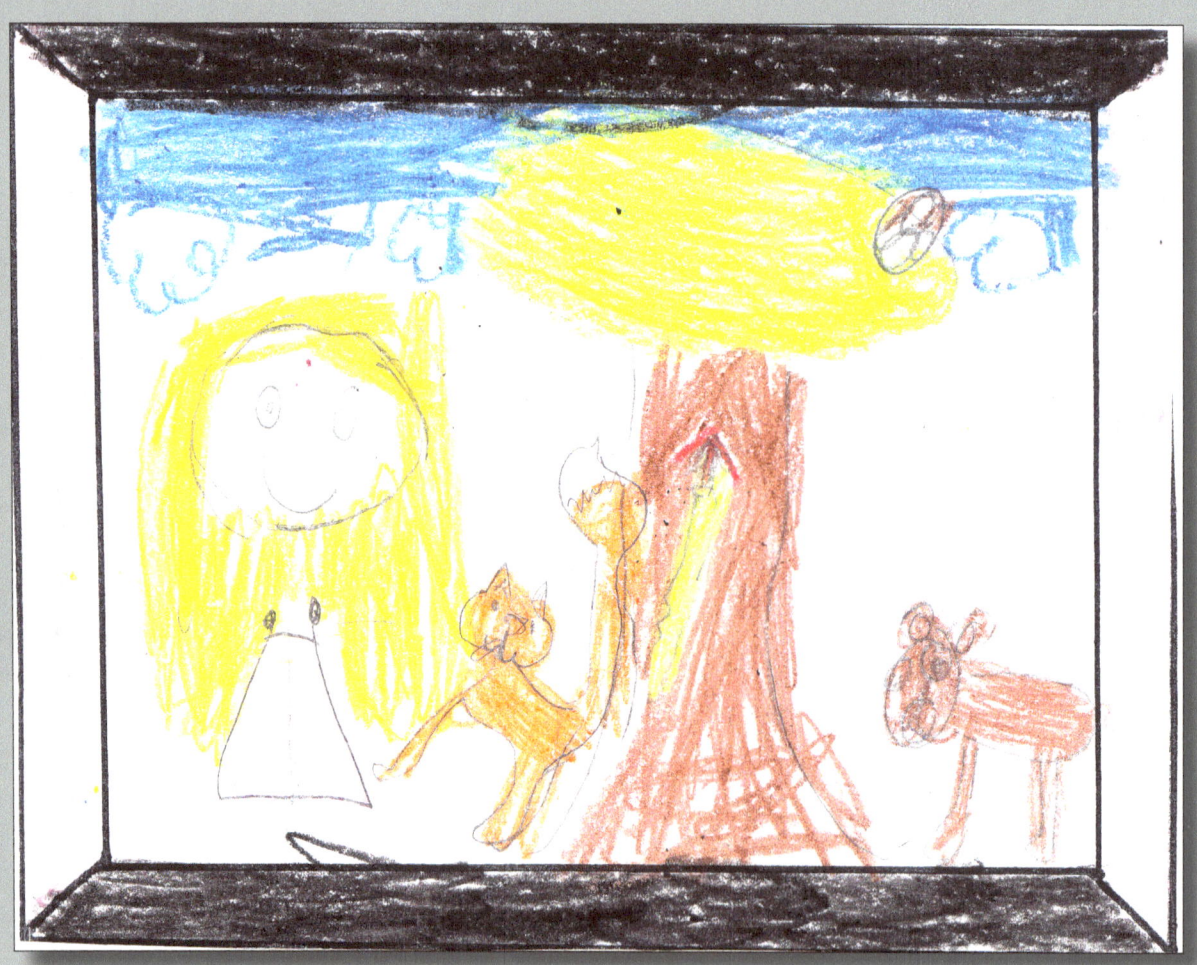

BY ALEXANDRIA

The WORLD WOULD be a better PLACE if...

it rained more (it has been very dry this year).

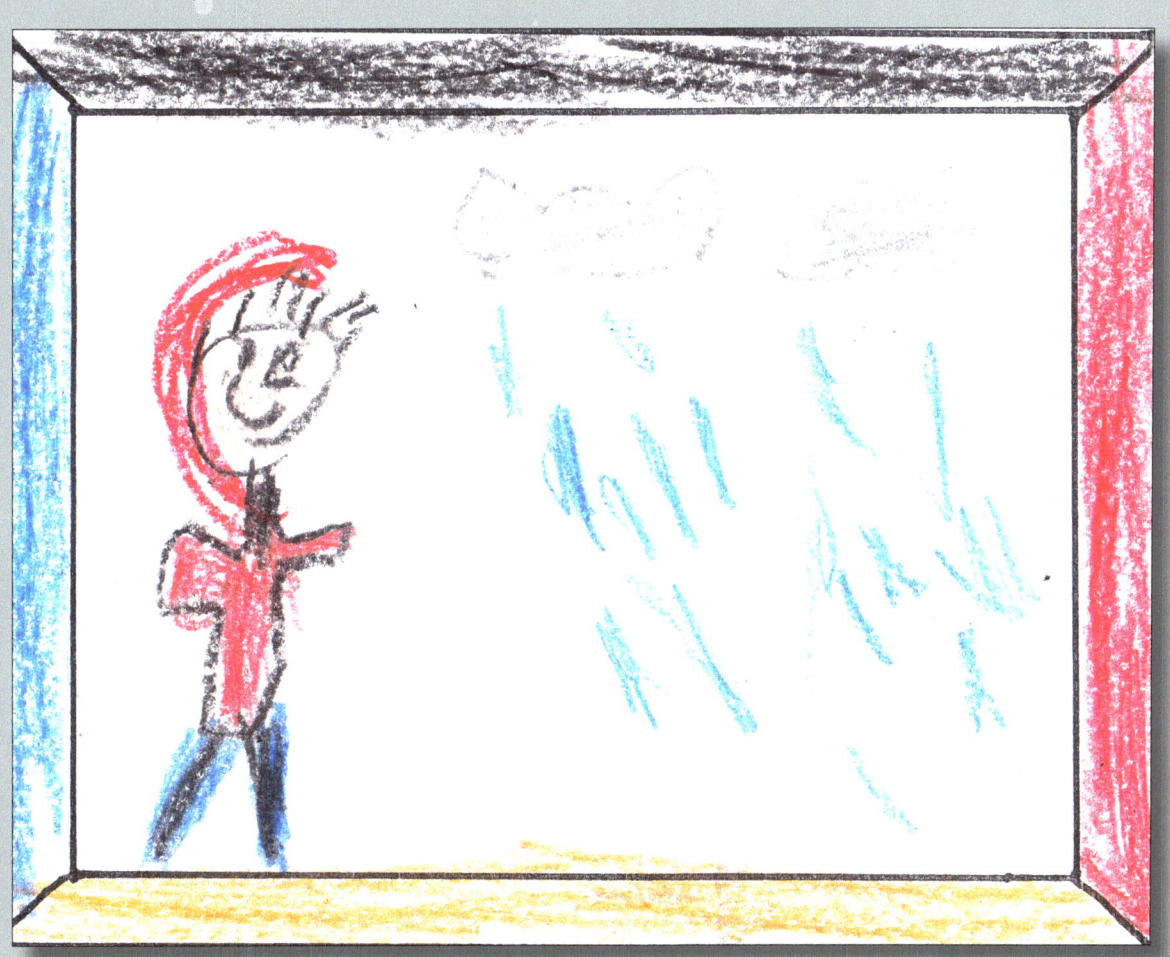

BY MATTHEW

The WORLD WOULD be a better PLACE if...

people had more time to rest.

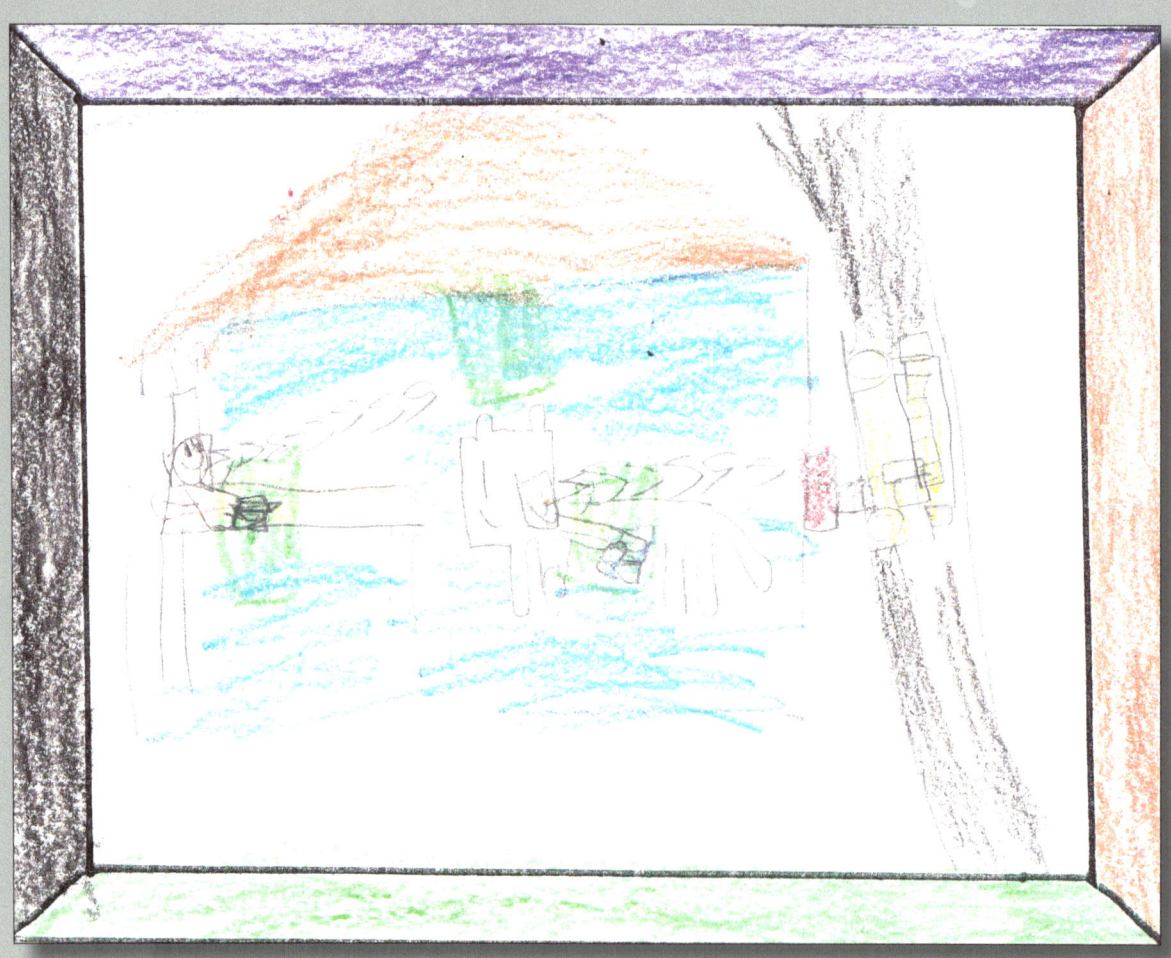

BY CHRIS

The WORLD WOULD be a better PLACE if...

the President gave people more stuff.

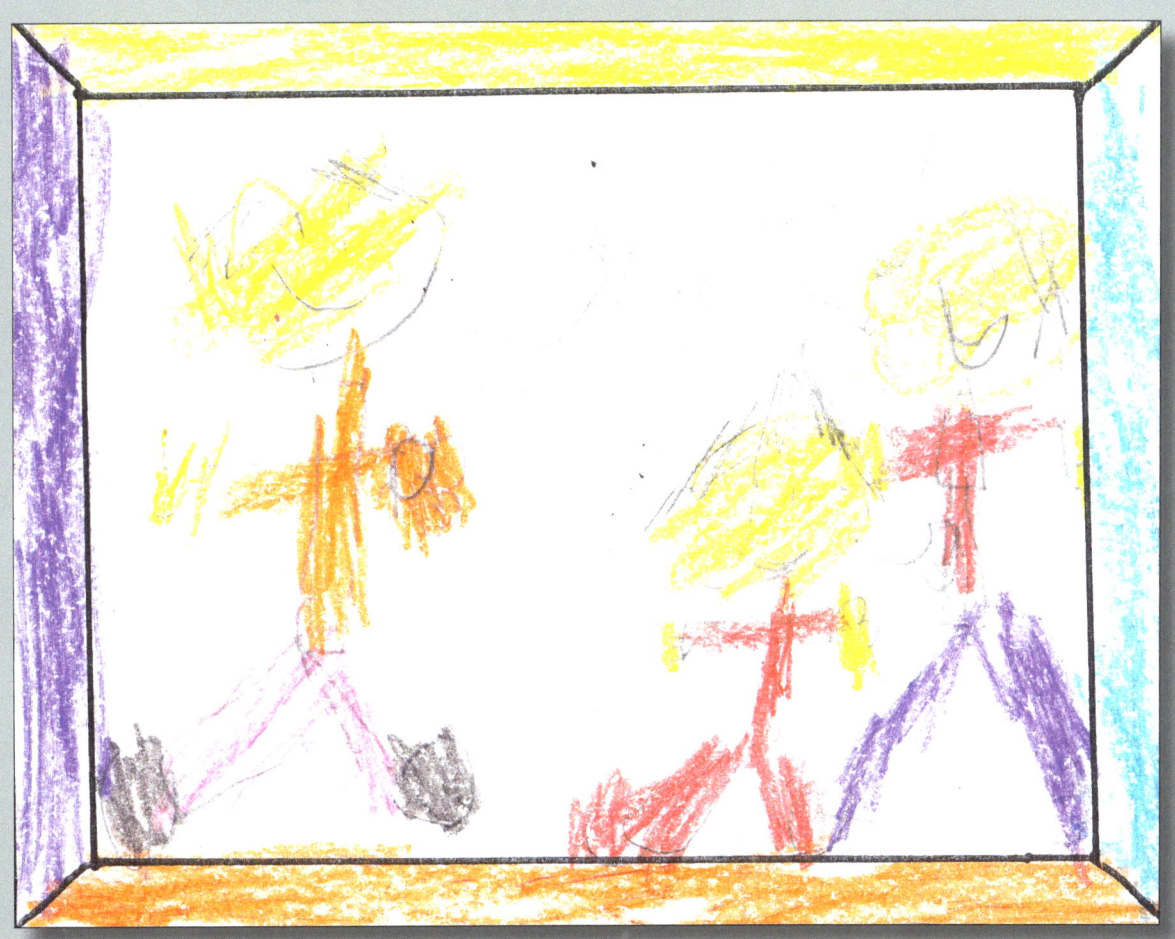

BY MARK

The WORLD WOULD be a better place if...

parents helped kids clean their room more.

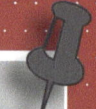

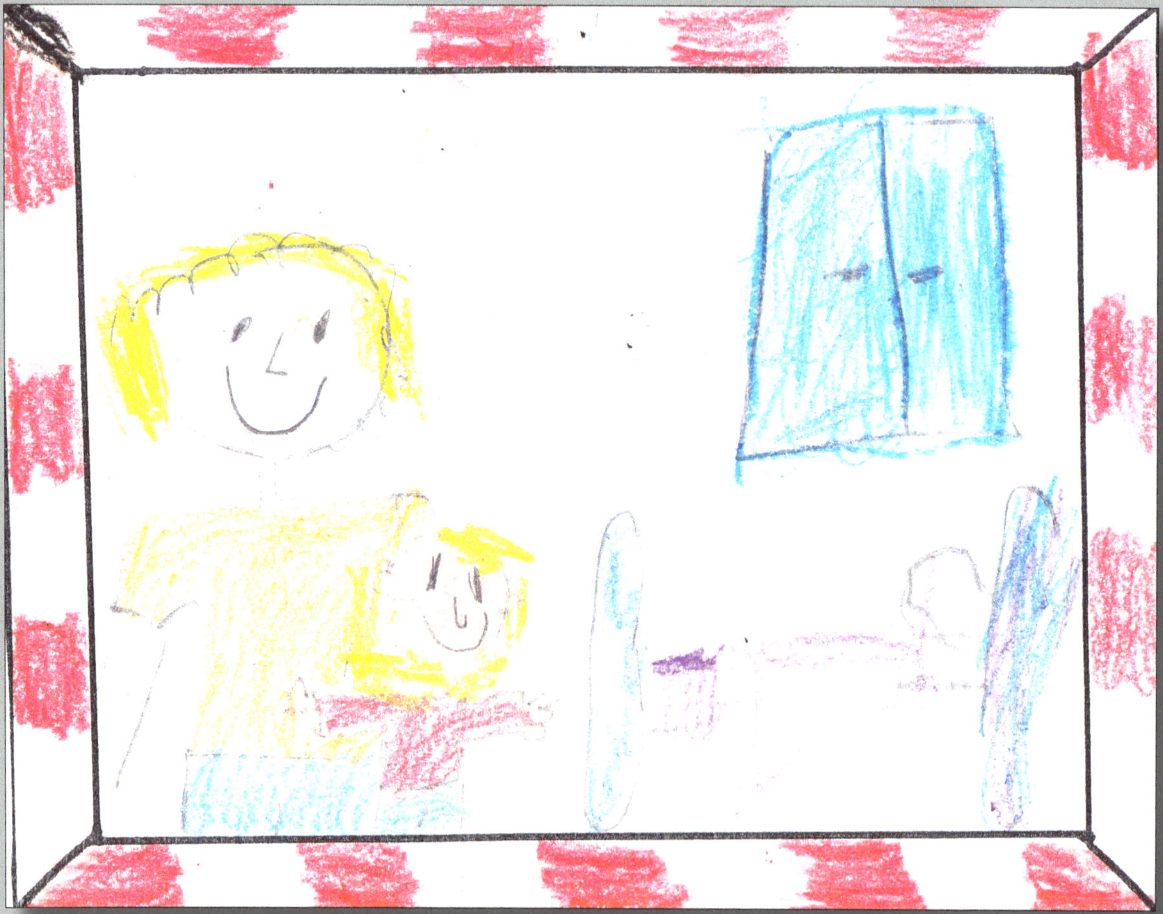

BY HANNAH

The WORLD WOULD be a better PLACE if...

we had breakfast with the principal every day.

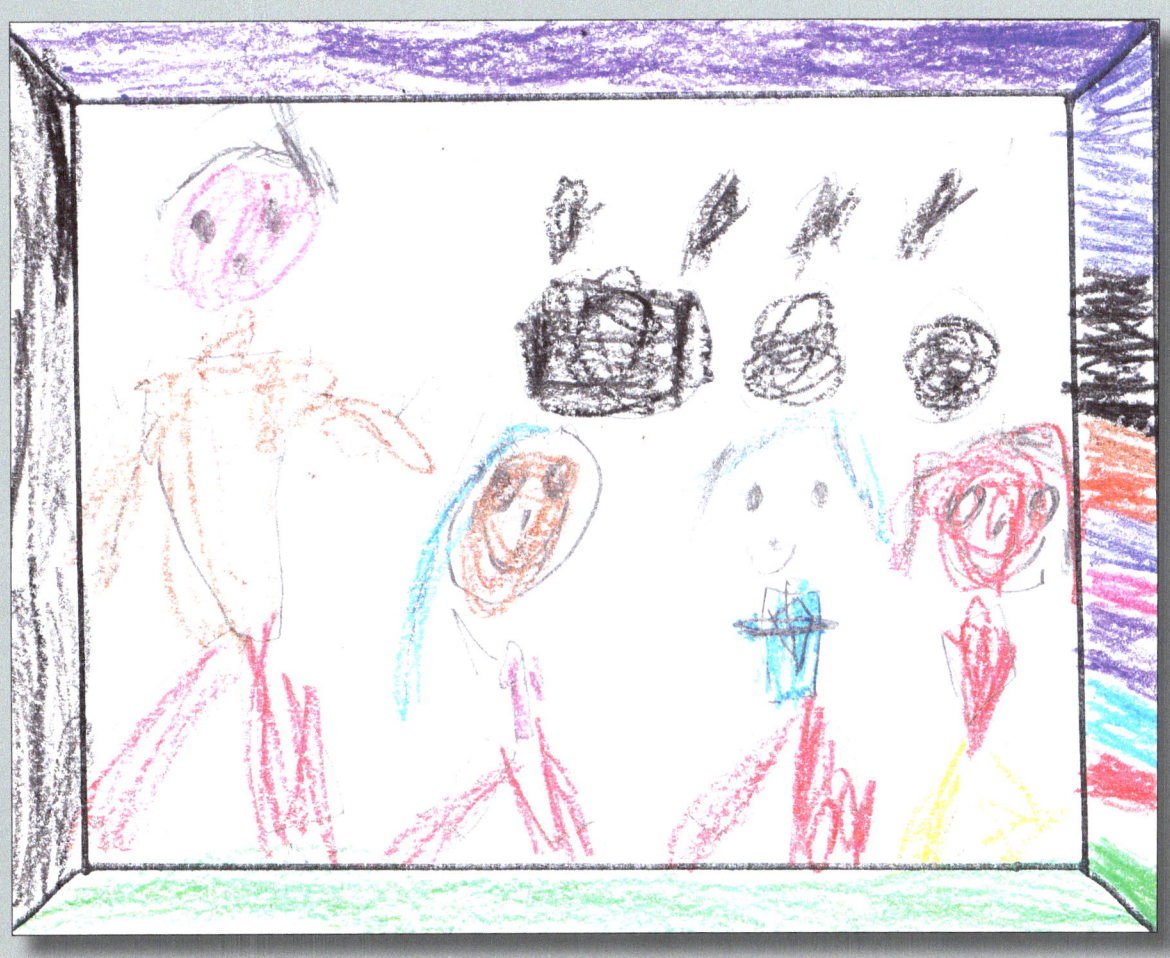

BY COOPER

The WORLD WOULD be a better PLACE if...

we had Pajama Day every day.

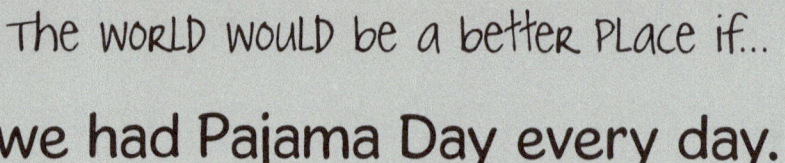

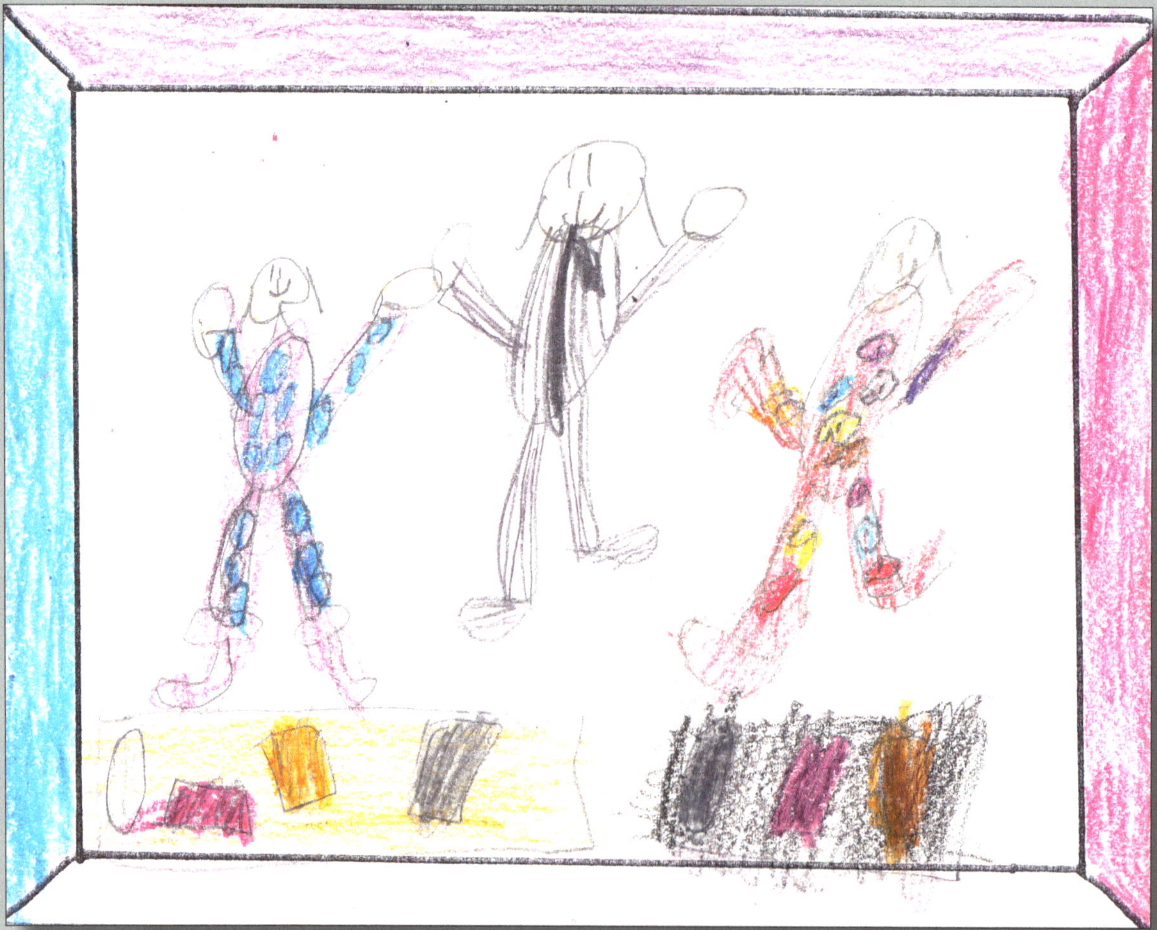

BY MAGGIE

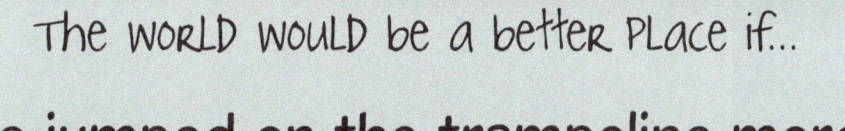

The WORLD WOULD be a better PLACE if...

we jumped on the trampoline more.

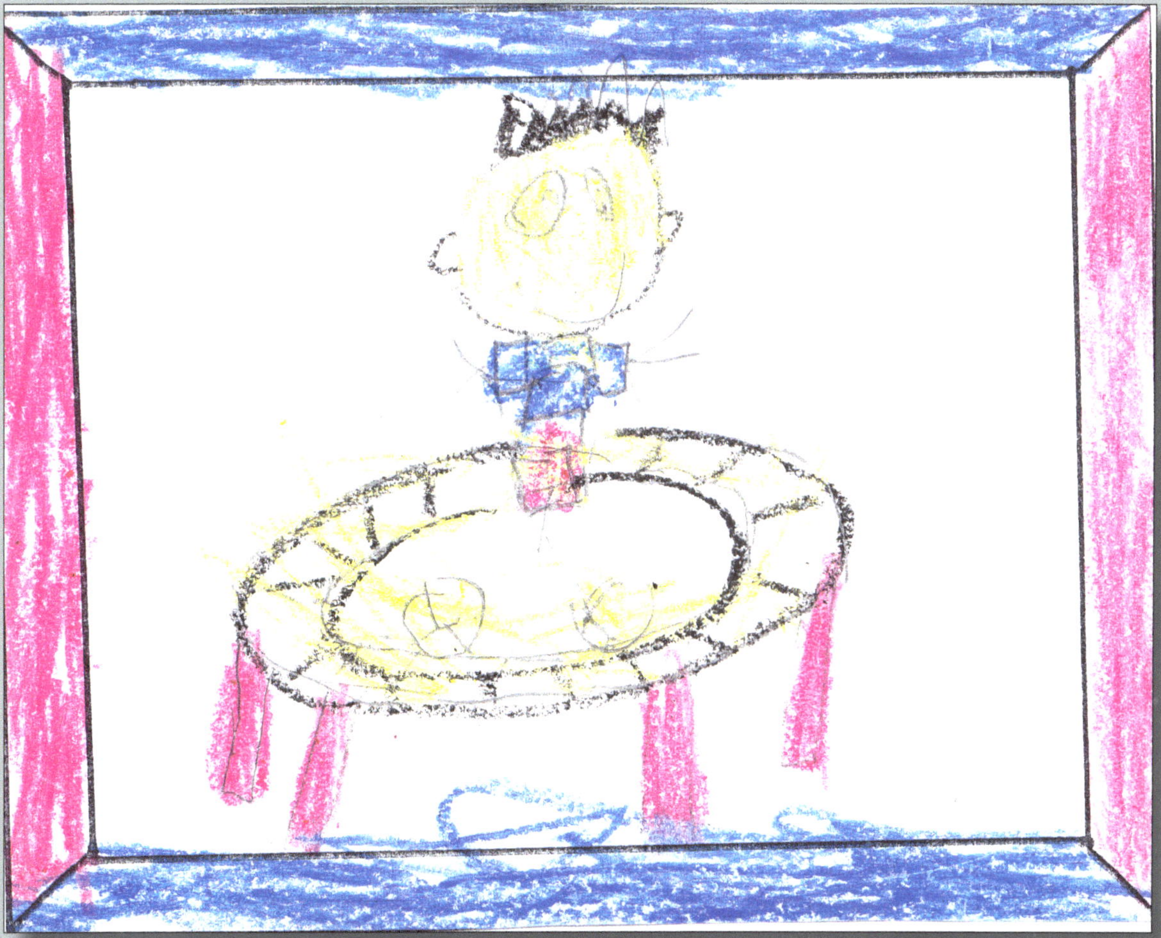

BY HUNTER

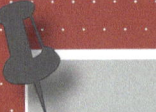
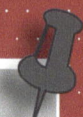

The WORLD WOULD be a better PLACE if...

adults were a little silly sometimes.

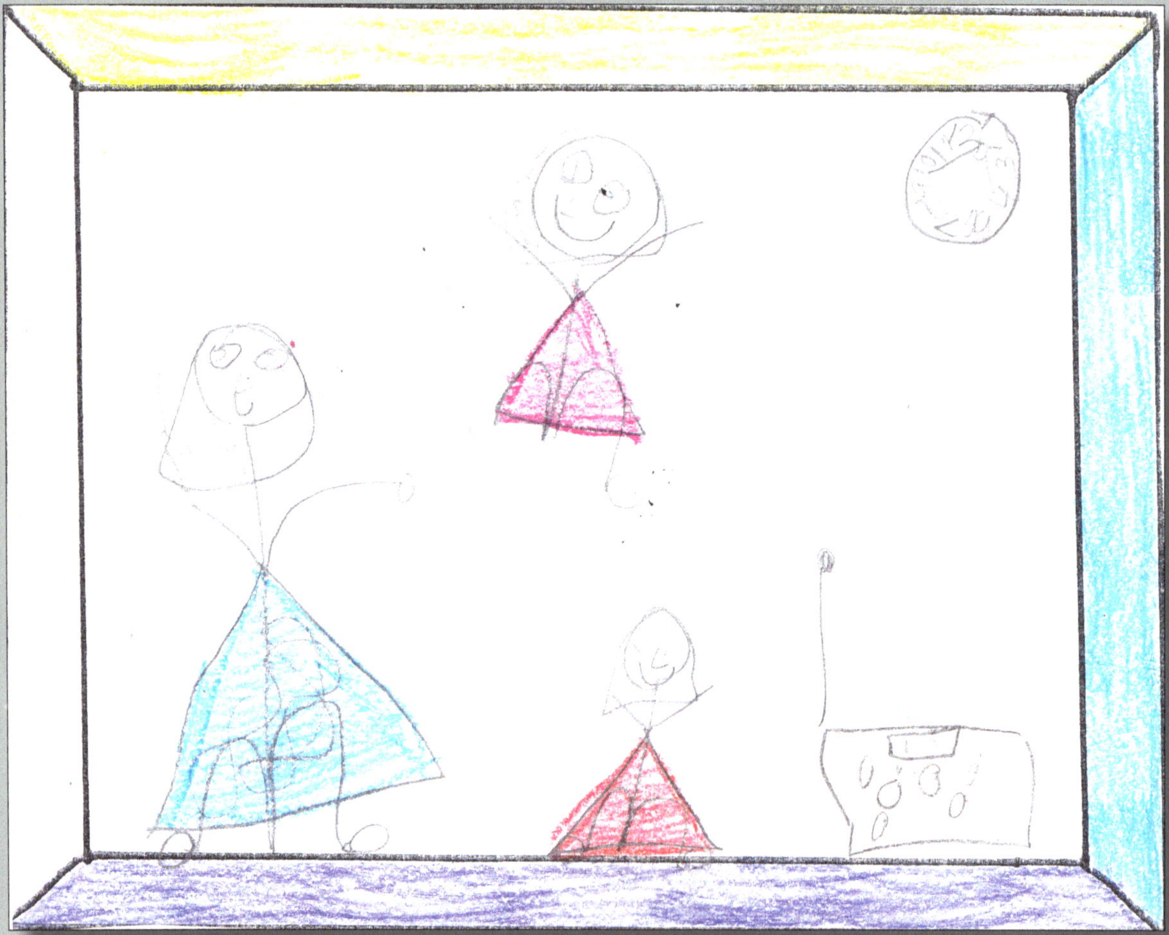

BY EMMA

The WORLD WOULD be a better PLACE if...

we exercised more.

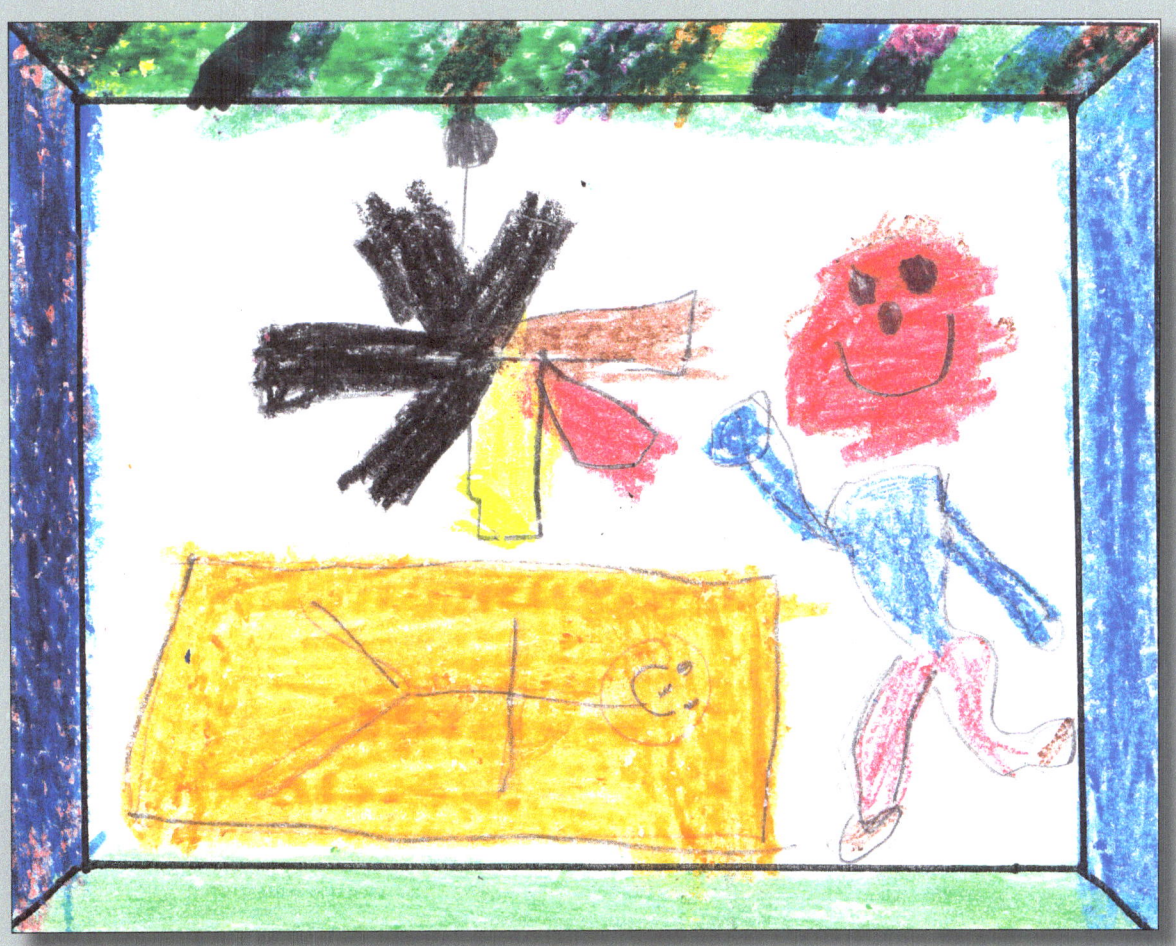

BY BRAEDEN

The WORLD WOULD be a better PLACE if...

teachers had sleepovers with kids.

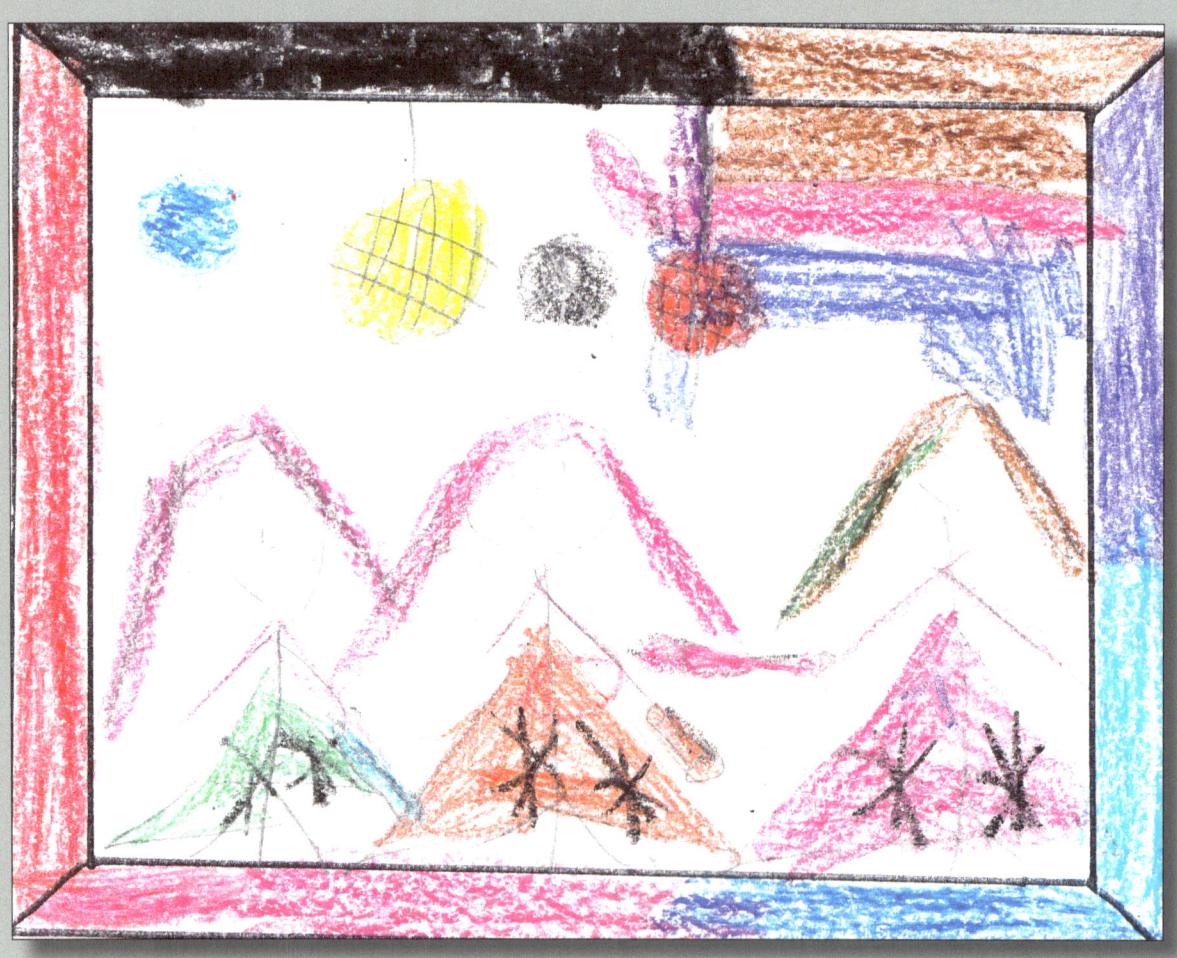

BY MEAGHAN

The WORLD WOULD be a better PLace if...

we did more science experiments.

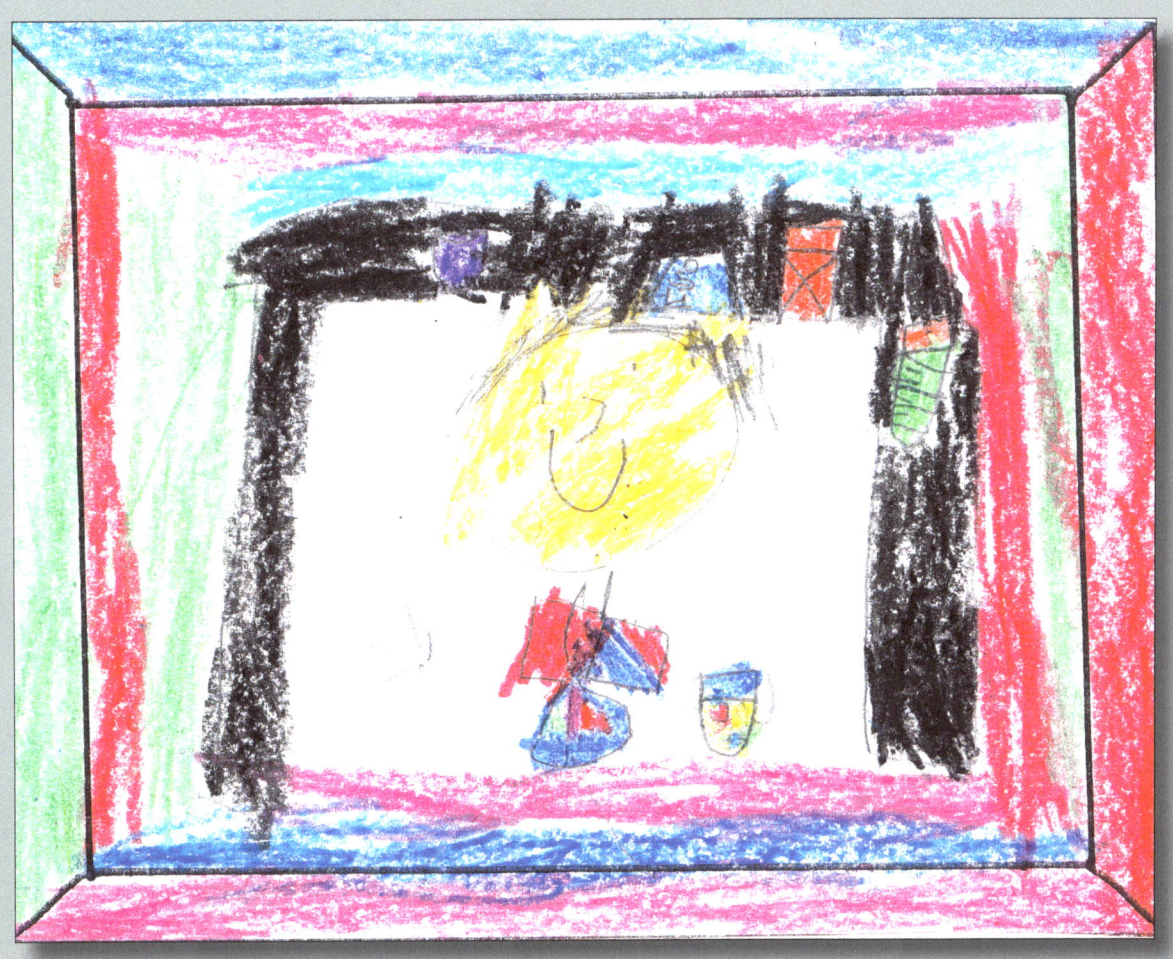

BY HOUSTON

The WORLD WOULD be a better PLACE if...

kids could stay up longer.

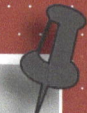

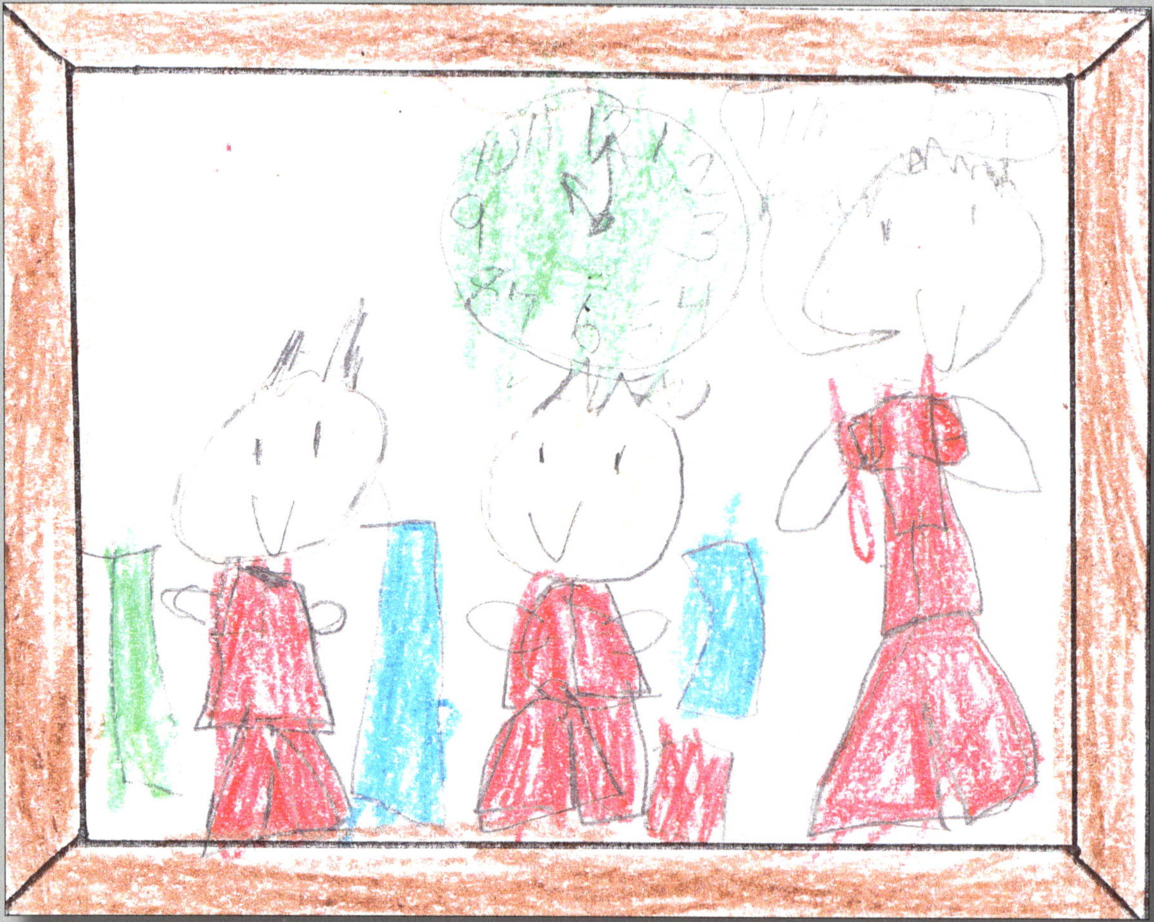

BY J.D. (JAMES)

The WORLD WOULD be a better PLACE if...

there were more of you in it.

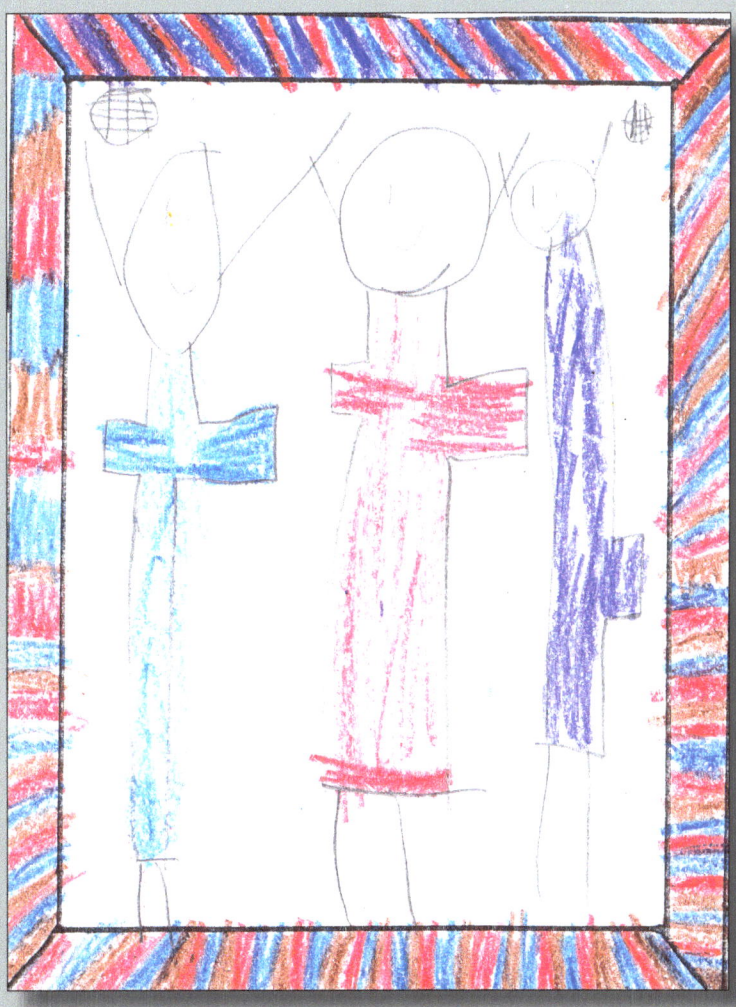

BY LEXI

Authors and Illustrators

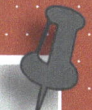

Matthew A.

Hunter A.

J.D. James A.

Cooper A.

Emma B.

Caleb B.

Houston B.

Cameron C.

Meaghan C.

Olivia D.

Hannah E.

Ethan G.

Ashley G.

Chris M.

Haley M.

Bella M.

Lexi N.

Maggie P.

Braeden P.

Alexandria R.

Mark S.

www.ingramcontent.com/pod-product-compliance
Lightning Source LLC
Chambersburg PA
CBHW050829200526
R18329200001B/R183292PG45159CBX00001B/1